PLAY MATTERS
so play as if it matters

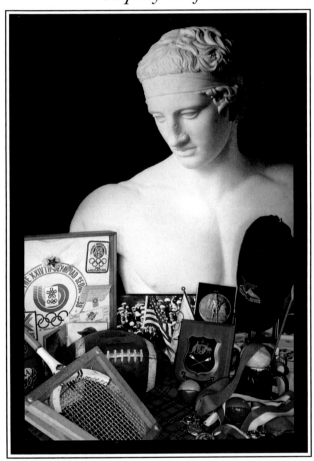

SUSAN SAINT SING, Ph.D.

vesuviuspress.com
AN IMPRINT OF TAU PUBLISHING, LLC

Play Matters
So Play As If It Matters
Susan Saint Sing, Ph.D.

Cover image: Susan Saint Sing
Cover and book design: Tau Publishing Design Department

For information regarding permission, write to:
Tau Publishing, LLC
Attention: Permissions Dept.
4727 North 12th Street
Phoenix, AZ 85014

ISBN 978-1-61956-086-4

First Edition January 2013
10 9 8 7 6 5 4 3 2 1

Published and printed in the United States of America by Vesuvius Press an imprint of Tau Publishing, LLC
For additional inspirational books visit us at TauPublishing.com

vesuviuspress.com

AN IMPRINT OF TAU PUBLISHING, LLC

DEDICATION

This book is dedicated to Dr. John Lucas, professor, Olympic historian, lecturer, and runner who was my teacher at the Pennsylvania State University when I was an undergraduate and later a member of my doctoral committee. He came in 3rd in the Rome 10,000 meter Olympic Trials and did not make the team. And he is forever remembered for his dedication to the Olympic movement and for having run his 10,000 meter race in every Olympic stadium in the world since 1960. He was a beloved educator, author, and lecturer worldwide as an official Olympic Historian.

Additionally, I dedicate this book to my friend, the venerable rower and coach, Ted Nash. Ted is an 11-time U.S. Olympic team member and in his career has a tally of 48 medals and 76 crews on the world and Olympic level. He started his Olympic rowing career in 1960 in Rome, winning a gold medal, and went on to win an Olympic bronze in 1964 Tokyo. He coached various rowing crews and medalists in these Olympic Games: 1968 Mexico, 1972 Munich, 1976 Montreal, 1988 Seoul, 1992 Barcelona, 1996 Atlanta, 2000 Sydney, 2004 Athens (gold-medal men's eight), and 2008 Beijing. No other coach from any nation has been a credentialed team member to more Olympic Games than Ted Nash. He is one of the finest men and greatest sportsmen and competitors I have ever known.

These men taught me the very best and highest values of sport and athletics and I am forever grateful for their time, mentoring, and friendship over the years. I would not have been able to write this book or achieve what I have achieved without them going before me and inspiring me with their goodness, humility, skill, and abundant knowledge and talent.

Were they ancient Greeks, statues would be chiseled in their honor, to stand at Olympia.

You are great athletes and even better human beings.
Thank you, I am always in your debt....

CONTENTS

Foreword
1

Introduction
3

Chapter One: The Energy of Play
7

Chapter Two: The Collective Kinetic Blueprint
17

Chapter Three: Breakthrough Kinesis
27

Chapter Four: *Agon* and the Hero Athlete
41

Chapter Five: Ectasy and the Hero Athlete
55

Chapter Six: Conclusion
63

Afterword
67

FOREWORD

Susan Saint Sing has written a book that is remarkable in scope—one that works to unify particle physics, play, the Divine … and everything in between. Relying heavily on the work of Carl Jung and his foundational theory of the collective unconscious, she addresses such topics as the universality of play, its remarkable powers of attraction, and its promise for a better future.

This is an ambitious book, reminiscent in some ways of the great unifying attempts made by Spinoza. Saint Sing describes the energetic dance of particles in string theory, in children bouncing balls, and in the cosmos itself. The content of this book will serve as an inspiration to those who love life, are ready to allow play to break out at a moment's notice, and see the Spirit lurking everywhere.

R. Scott Kretchmar, Ph.D.
The Pennsylvania State University

INTRODUCTION

Over the past 15 years, I have been asked to frame my ideas in books, magazine articles, journals, international conferences, and at the Vatican about play and the energy which urges us to play. As a national team athlete, a 7-time national medal winning coach, and a Ph.D., the fundamental question of *why* we play, followed by the secondary question of *why do we play to such extremes*—as on the elite level—has intrigued me.

In this book, *Play Matters*, I intend to look at play over a continuum of time, over many disciplines and across various discourse communities, from children to elite athletes, from its origins to the present. Why? Because another consideration that fascinates me is that anthropologists tell us that play is the one consistent aspect of all cultures, both historically and globally. This speaks to me of some type of universal qualities of play that our human nature has within it. I see these aspects as being both physical and spiritual—the "handedness and footedness" that we know and experience in the everyday and the more ethereal quality of the inner need, the drive to express and experience play in games and sport to the highest limit of "self"—the search of that which is beyond the physical boundary.

In order to explore play I will be examining how play is described by scientists and poets, Nobel Laureates, etc. I believe there is an energy of play that is linked to the energy of the expanding universe—and that is why play is found in all cultures, in all ages. I think we are "hard-wired" to play in our physical and mental make-up and that

3

there is a collective kinetic imprint within us—similar to the idea of the collective unconscious as described by the eminent psychiatrist Carl Jung. Our science of play is anchored in some of the greatest social movers of humankind: the Olympic Games, the World Cup, the World Series, Super Bowl, etc. We make heroes of people who can ride a bike fast. *Why do we do it?* Why do they choose to go through that wall of pain? Why do we honor them? What is it we are seeking? These are the types of questions this book will address.

I believe there is a substantial depth to play, games, and sport that has its origins in ancient myths, the collective unconscious, and the very energy of the origins of the universe. It is my hope that this book will fill a void in the present literature and examine, chapter by chapter, these ideas so that the classroom teachers, practitioners, coaches, trainers, and athletes themselves can better understand—and therefore gain insight to better performance—*why* we play looking at the question from an unconscious, energy perspective. For if we can gain this understanding, and we can examine and name consistent trends, then we can expand the envelope of possibility and contribute to the advancement of humankind. *Play matters, so we should play as if it matters.* I see this in several layers and it is my hope that I can communicate, as I try to "peel away the onion" and get to the heart of what and why play is. "Play matters" is intended to be read with several implied meanings. One meaning is to see it as—*play matters*, read as—play is important. The other way I intend is for this book to look into what I think are several aspects of *play matters*, read as—issues pertaining to play, similar to the saying "family matters." Additionally, there is a layer that is the physical *play matter*—the physiological cellular level leading into the atomic level of energy. And interfacing with all of these levels is the human kinetic blueprint that collectively initiates, participates and preserves play in the collective unconscious. This embedded human condition bubbles within. It is recognized and shared and spread among us just as Woodstock vicariously and serendipitously poured out from an unconscious need of a generation to gather and "be" the gushing outpouring truth of their generation.

4

Play is part of us and we carry its collective kinetic blueprint always. It inspires, astounds, delights, and challenges. And it is always instantly recognized when it breaks out in a moment of perfection. You don't need a rule book or a diagram when that gut stopping moment occurs as when Fosbury did his first flop and revolutionized high jumping, when Shaun White snow-boarded down a mountain, doing 3 dimensional tricks along a spiral axis at break-neck speed in a half-pipe for Olympic gold, or when Torvel and Dean ice-danced their interpretation of Bolero to earn a perfect 6.0 from all judges in the 1984 Olympics. But is there more to it?

These moments of time-stopping executions of perfection are instantly recognized in the gut. Humans stop and "ooh and ahh" at greatness. We hold our breath until the diver or the skater or the gymnast executes the final twist or turn that punctuates a perfect 10 and then we collectively applaud and jump to our feet because *we are part of it.* In a way, I will dare to say that we have in fact participated in it and helped its execution along to be brought forth at this time at this moment, because we have a collective kinetic relationship to one another along the continuum of human existence. And it is toward this end, of revealing these layers, that this book is dedicated in my humble attempt to take the simple action of a child bouncing a ball—and tie it to the cosmos.

CHAPTER ONE

THE ENERGY OF PLAY
FOLLOWING A THREAD ALONG A CONTINUUM[1]

This opening chapter will examine the very energy—the impulse within us which urges us to play. It will examine questions across different discourse communities and historical perspectives on why we play. This chapter will consider this broad-based thread of expression in terms of play, energy, and the origins of the universe. We will look at many questions such as: Is there a reason—hardwired within us—to play? Is the energy of play linked to the physical universe? What do physicists say about play on the atomic level? There has been much speculation in physics on the origins of the universe, string theory, and the understanding of the ethereal fabric of which we are made. Can we link this energy, this fabric that pertains to the essence of matter and energy in the universe which includes the human imprint in a continuum from the moment of the origin of the universe, to the modern athlete and beyond? For if this energy continuum can be seen as plausible, then it fills a gap and aids the modern sport philosopher in understanding how the impetus to play within the element of sport helps us transcend our base nature, and advance humankind as part of the energy of the expanding universe.

To answer these questions we will jump around a bit through the ages, and examine some of ideas of the greatest thinkers. To begin, let us consider that scientists, mathematicians, poets, theologians,

---

1 Parts of this chapter were given in a talk at the Inaugural International Conference for Sport and Spirituality at York St. Johns University, England. Additionally, selections of this chapter were first printed by Routledge Press, Nov. 2010 in *Theology, Ethics and Transcendence in Sports*. Edited by Nick Watson, Jim Parry, Mark Stephen Nesti.

and artists all reflect, name, and describe—energy—as part of the moment of creation, as part of the essence and the intention of the Creator. It would not be uncommon to find science considering energy. Energy is certainly expressed in the arts and humanities—so let us examine how energy and God are used together across all these disciplines.

A cornerstone in these explorations are key, pivotal ideas such as Carl Jung's insight and description of a collective unconscious. Jung describes a collective unconscious which carries primordial archetypes—foci of energy—that issue forth as images and symbols, which influence all people through the ages along the continuum. This collective unconscious is akin to a collective knowledge, passed from generation to generation since the inception of humankind's origins. Reflections of this collective unconscious reveal themselves to us through the images and symbols by which we name things, identify things, and describe things—a common thread. (Some Christians might see a comparison relative to this psychological term in the Communion of Saints or the Body of Christ.) These reflections stem from archetypes of the unconscious which include the trickster, the mother, and the hero. According to Jung, archetypes create myths, religions, and philosophical ideas that influence and set their stamp on whole nations and epochs.[2] Since sport is one of the largest social movers in the world, would archetypes not influence and set their stamp on play and sport?

Considering the above—if, through the ages, and across these planes and levels of competition a broad discourse of people: writers, scientists, theologians, philosophers, artists, all speak in similar terms of experience—they are probably reflecting more than just their opinion, they are probably expressing, or being moved to express, a similar unifying human understanding. According to psychiatrist Alexander A. Weech, Jung's theory of the collective unconscious can be looked upon as this type of dynamic. In this collective understanding then, can we recognize descriptions and images of

---

2   Carl Jung, from his writings 1956.

play that give us clues to the origins of the energy of play? That link us, and place us in a continuum with the moment of the creation of the universe—and therefore with the Creator? Let us take a journey along the continuum and across several disciplines and see....

What do some Nobel Laureates in physics say about energy, creation, and God? One of the greatest thinkers about the universe is Albert Einstein. He wrote volumes. Throughout his lifetime he was asked to expand on his thoughts of God and the universe in both physics and philosophical thought. Einstein never accepted that the universe was governed by chance but by immutable laws. One of his popular quotes about which much has been written is, "God does not play dice." He said about energy that, "Energy evolved in very regular ways." It had purpose.[3]

So how did the universe evolve? Continuing with thinking about the origins of the universe, what about the first moment of creation— the first moment of when energy was sent forth? Leon Lederman, a Nobel Laureate in physics calls this moment of pre-existence a time of the, "God Particle.... We don't know anything about the universe until it reaches the mature age of a billionth of a trillionth of a second."[4] Stephen Hawking infers that God is something of a mathematical necessity for the universe to exist under the laws which it does. [5] That Hawking infers a "necessity" for God is not entirely new. Earlier, along the continuum, in 1250 C.E., Aquinas describes aspects of God—goodness, necessity, intelligence—in collective terms as "understood by all," aspects which "everyone understands to be God."[6] Perhaps Hawking is expanding on Aquinas' insights through the collective unconscious.

At the moment of creation in order for the near instantaneous creation of the known universe to exist, there was a burst of energy that

3   Albert Einstein, Letter to Max Born (4 December 1926); *The Born-Einstein Letters* (Translated by Irene Born) (Walker and Company, new York, 1971.)

4   Leon Lederman, *The God Particle: If the Universe is the Answer What is the Question?* (New York: Houghton Mifflin Company, 1993) 1.

5   Stephen Hawking, *A Briefer History of Time* (New York: Bantam Publishing, 2005).

6   Thomas Aquinas, *The Summa Theologica*.

formed the matter and antimatter that many physicists now believe consists of "strings." String theory is very complicated but it consists of a way of expressing the smallest particles of energy that exists in all parts and circumstances of the universe, thus perhaps providing a unifying theory between quantum physics and Newtonian physics. Physicist Brian Greene states, "According to string theory we would find that each [particle] is not point-like, but instead, consists of a loop…each particle contains an oscillating, vibrating, dancing filament."[7]

With strings we have energy likely to be present in all matter and antimatter, present in good energy and dark energy that is "described" and "recognized" by scientists in the language of play as—dancing. Interesting! Going back to Jung, If we describe what we "see," what we recognize, and name based on previous learning models and experience, stemming from the collective past, then the physicist, Greene, who was moved to describe the energy of strings as dancing, might be identifying this movement as so because it strikes a chord, memory, some visual link to a past occurrence where energy danced, where energy was intended and was part of the fabric and the very essence of the Creator.

What do the poets say? Poets are always trying to succinctly distil the thoughts of their time and can perhaps help illuminate us even more. The consummate poet and wisdom-figure Dante writes, "Thus, even as he wheeled to his own music, I saw that substance sing, that spirit-flame above whom double lights were twinned; and he and his companions moved within their dance…"[8] The modern period T. S. Eliot writes, "Except for the point, the still point, there would be no dance, and there is only the dance. I can only say there we have been: but I cannot say where."[9] What is Eliot seeing in his mind when he writes that there is a still point without which

---

7   Brian Greene, *The Elegant Universe* (New York: Vintage Books, 2000) 14.

8   Disappearance of the Roman Emperor Justinian and his fellow spirits in the wake of hymning and dancing, *The Divine Comedy*, Dante Alighieri, "Paradiso," Canto VII 4:7.

9   T.S. Eliot, *The Four Quartets*.

there would be no dance – what is this "still point" out of which and around which all things dance? Is it God? Or the Trinity, or is he perhaps referring to Aristotle's Prime Mover?

What do the theologians say of the dance and the still point? St. Bonaventure states that the love of the Trinity is like a dance, its love is so great it becomes creation.[10] Aquinas says, "Therefore it is necessary to arrive at a first mover, put in motion by no other; and this everyone understands to be God."[11] The still point is the beginning, the moment just before Creation, after which everything is in motion. Do we have any idea of what this moment of creation was like? Are there any clues that there was a moment in eternity through which the beginning of time passed? In our brief look thus far at eminent thinkers can we continue and link what the poets and theologians are talking about with science? Yes! Astrophysicist Neil de Grasse Tyson, in his book on the universe entitled *Origins* states that cosmic background radiation (CBR) carries the imprint of a portal through which all of us once passed.[12]

Dare we call this portal the moment of creation? What do the artists show us about this? Is it represented in Michelangelo's "touch" between God and Adam on the ceiling of the Sistine Chapel? Is this what he is creating from his collective unconscious? If the Creator loosed this energy in the universe setting forces in motion, is one of the energies on this imprint the urge to play? Is play part of the fabric of God?

What does scripture tell us? The first book of Genesis tells us that Adam and Eve were made in God's image.[13] Adam and Eve were made according to God's likeness, does this likeness include play? Scripture tells us, "When he set the heavens in their place I was there, when he girdled the ocean....Then I was at his side each day, his darling and delight, playing in his presence continually, playing on

10   St. Bonaventure, *Collected Works*.

11   Ibid., Aquinas.

12   Neil de Grasse Tyson and Donald Goldsmith, *Origins* W.W. Norton and Company New York 2004.

13   Genesis 1:26, 27.

the earth, when he had finished it…."[14]

We have looked at physicists, theologians, poets, scripture, and psychotherapists—what do philosophers say about this energy of play? What is play? Let us start first with the modern, renowned sport philosophers R. Scott Kretchmar and Johan Huizinga who say play is a "state of fundamental pre-rational spontaneity which is freely chosen and entered into for the simple sake of wanting to do so. It is of a nature outside of the reality of the present, yet is equally as real to the player or players as the present is to an observer…"[15] This description contains many of the elements and experience of the spiritual, doesn't it?

Play can take many forms, as many forms as any individual or group of individuals fancies entering into. Since physicist Brian Greene used the image of energy dancing as when describing strings, let us examine the example of play as dancing and see what the collective body of knowledge might be telling us.

'He who cannot dance is not educated.' Said Plato with epigrammatic terseness in just two short words, "*achoreutos apaideutos.*"[16] The Ancient Greeks were obsessed with the body beautiful. Education consisted of the intellectual ones' study of music and dance, and the physical. The balance of body and soul. Dancing was considered in such high regard that Xenophon considered it a scientific system to train the entire body symmetrically. Grace in play was held in high regard in ancient Greece in poetry, captured on vases, written in Homer's Odyssey. Homer took time to immortalize ball playing on a beach by Princess Nausicaa and her handmaiden, whose movements Homer likens to the grace of a goddess and further, a similar game played by two male youths Halias and Laodamas

---

14 Proverbs 8: 27-31.

15 Morgan and Meier, *Philosophic Inquiry in Sport*, (Champaign, IL: Human Kinetics, 1995).

16 Ronald A. Smith and James G. Thompson, editors, *History of sport and Physical Activity: An Anthology* (Department of Kinesiology, The Pennsylvania State University, 1998), 35.

whom Homer specifically points out were unrivaled dancers.[17] Two thousand years later, again in present day, the sport philosopher, Johan Husizinga, echoes a similar appreciation: "The connections between playing and dancing are so close that they hardly need illustrating. It is not that dance has something of play in it or about it, rather it is an integral part of play: the relationship is one of direct participation, almost of essential identity...dancing is a particular and particularly perfect form of playing."[18] Dance, being an integral part of play, a perfect form of play is also a prime example of play and should therefore be reflected throughout the collective unconscious.

If the impetus to play is from the Creator, it would have to have been there since the beginning. So when does the impetus, the intention, the energy to play come in? Has it always been with humankind? What do the anthropologists say? In her book, *Dancing in the Streets*, Barbara Ehrenreich says that anthropologists conclude that all civilizations have recorded play of some sort.[19] Thus, continuum of play is part of our historical collective fiber.

For the spiritual being what comes before civilization as we know it? The Garden—the Garden of Eden, a time when we were one with God. Does/did play exist there? Well, one could argue that if we are in God, and God is in us, and we are in one another, and since we are never outside of the omnipresent God, then the Garden is always present to us which prompts us, collectively, to move toward play. Moreover, there is historical evidence for this because playfulness is throughout scripture in the Judeo-Christian tradition. What else does scripture say? Let us consider God arguing creation with Job: "Can you lead about the crocodile with a hook? Can you play with him (crocodile) as with a bird?" And, "...Strength is lodged in his neck and untiring energy dances ahead of him (the crocodile)."[20] And again, "Here ships ply their course; here Leviathan your creature

17 Ibid.
18 Johan Husizinga, *Homo Ludens* (London: Routledge and Kegan Press, 1950), 165.
19 Ehrenreich, Barbara, *Dancing in the Streets: A History of Collective Joy* (New York: Henry Holt and Company, 2006).
20 *New American Bible*, Job 40:29 and Job 41:22.

which you formed plays, "...your creature Leviathan which you formed to play...." [21] Three examples of play have thus far been shown to be centered in the spiritual: God playing with creation; God forming things to play; God describing this energy of play as dancing. Thus far we have looked at modern science, modern and ancient philosophers, but with the exception of Dante we skipped over the middle. What about the Middle Ages?

There are various examples of toys and games, sports stemming from the Middle Ages up through to modern time. We know that play as far back as the Ancient Olympics has been associated with religion and at times even spirituality. In the Middle Ages, a time of weighted existence for humankind, beset with plague and war and struggle—did play have its place in advancing and elevating us?

One of the remarkable figures of the Middle Ages was St. Francis. Movies have been written about his short but poignant life. Son of a wealthy cloth merchant, knight, prisoner of war, guest of a Pope, stigmatized saint and founder of one of the world's largest religious orders, St. Francis of Assisi might not be the obvious personage in whom to look for play. However, Victor Turner considered St. Francis, this 13th century mystic, as one of the most profound examples of the liminal man. Francis, though considered a serious ascetic, was also known to be whimsical. Legends repeatedly tell of his playful nature which is often portrayed with birds and animals about him. In his austere poverty in seeking closeness to God he himself is recorded as playing a mystical violin throughout the countryside—joyfully playing with and among creation. So in this one example from the Middle Ages, a dark time in the continuum, we see *a legend* reaching out to us moderns from the past from those remembered, not only for his asceticism but also for *his play*. Astounding.

So we see that all cultures play. There are myriad examples and styles of play through the ages. Humans play. Even animals play. Play is part of the fabric of God's creative energy.

Play could be considered an invitation passing back and forth

---

21   *Holman Christian Standard Bible*, Psalm 104:26.

between the energy of God and the energy here in this world's creation. We engage when the urge to play comes upon us, we, like children, respond to it in glee—and then it is gone for a time. The response, the communion, is returned and exchanged with and to the Creator until the next time. We have within our power the will to engage or refuse that Presence; and in the refusal we lapse into the shadow of our darker nature. What is it that unites body, mind, and soul into the mind/body/soul? What is the "body electric" that poet and philosopher Walt Whitman talks about? What is it that we know when something greater is there, out there on the field, or in the gym? What we are responding to is the experience of grace. A human effort has been graced by God. We, in our creaturehood, having come from the Creator, and still being enlivened by the energy and spirit of the Creator—inherently respond to this communion—it resonates with a template within us. The template is the memory or recognition of godliness. Play is a return to that, a memory pushing through layers of consciousness and breaking surface like a wave on a beach where we like children, press our toes in the sand for a moment and then it is gone, to resurface later. Play is an archetype of goodness and joy, a cluster of energy mirroring the last memories of the perfect human state and union with God—a momentary return to the Garden of Eden.[22]

---

22 Segments of this last paragraph were first published in *Spirituality of Sport: Balancing Body and Soul* published by St. Anthony Messenger Press, Cincinnati, OH, 2004.

CHAPTER TWO

THE COLLECTIVE KINETIC BLUEPRINT

Play and its relationship to games and sports share a rich contribution to myth, culture, and tradition all along the historic continuum from primitive to modern societies. Morgan and Meier in their esteemed text *Philosophic Inquiry in Sport* tell us that as moderns our, "games re-enact cosmic and social dramas whose meaning have long been forgotten; the wish for heavenly conquest becomes the greasy pole, football, the titanic struggle between opposing forces over possession of the solar globe...." [23]

In the American southwest petrogylphs we see Anasazi flute-dancer images of Kokopelli etched in rocks from ancient times. From nomads in the Sahara desert to Himalayan Sherpas, people preserve their culture through ritual dances, masks, toys for children, musical instruments, dice and games.

There is no doubt that play, games and sport have left a huge historical impact. They have been and are a *big* deal culturally. Ancient Olympiads impacted their world substantially with cease-fires from war, lavish monetary awards to victors, heightened times of celebration and trade Our sports today are literally more global yet similarly are vast social and economic movers. According to the prestigious British magazine, *The Spectator*, in an illuminating article about sports, it is estimated that, "the global sports market is worth around 500 billion pounds sterling a year."[24] That's about 800

---

23 William J. Morgan and Klaus V. Meier, editors, *Philosophic Inquiry in Sport* (Champaign, IL: Human Kinetics Press, 1988), 114.

24 "The Spectator," 4 Feb 2012, 34.

billion U.S. dollars! This incredible amount of money innervates economies and can drive sociocultural trends. Sport scintillates our imaginations as in the Hollywood films, *Seabiscut* and *Invictus*, and elevates individuals like Michael Jordan and Tiger Woods to super human status and wealth. Sport has been credited for nation building; it certainly pervades (invigorates) international relations in such historical competitions as the America's Cup and Wimbledon.

Spontaneous play evolves into rules and measured games which develop into competitive, highly organized sports. And through this thread of play which runs through these three aspects of human action we create icons. Through play we create our sports heroes, propagating the hero athlete for our period of time on the historical continuum and moving the myth into the next generation of the collective unconscious that will benefit from our advances of the kinetic blueprint, and ultimately we are unifying, polishing, amalgamating—hopefully toward a higher plane. Play, games and sport are integral to the human experience. If we are not directly involved then we have been impacted by them. Play has intrigued humankind and been integral to the human condition in all its forms since we first existed.

Moreover we are physical beings. We have handedness and footedness. Movement is intrinsic to our existence. Dance is an elevation of our movement. And play is a seminal impetus to dance. So what do biologists and physiologists say about energy and play? Do we benefit from the handedness and footedness of one another? Have we benefited from the handedness and footedness of our ancestors? Do we excel more as we follow the continuum?

Clearly, times in the mile or the 100-meter dash get faster and faster as the decades go on. Does our collective unconscious include a collective kinetic unconscious that is evolving from millennia to millennia? Since we are not just mind or spirit but body too, it would seem to follow that a collective unconscious would have to prompt a collective kinetic inclusion. We seek to express what has not been expressed before. We seek to execute gymnastic tricks that have a higher degree of difficulty than in a previous competition so we are awarded more points for the attempt to advance the sport. Ice skating judges were thrilled with the first single jump, and now a triple isn't good enough for Olympic gold. Surely there is a collective drive to perfect the body movement, look, function.

Carl Jung states that, we are born with a psychological as well as a biological heritage. The collective unconscious, which results from experiences that are common to all people, also includes material from our pre-human and animal ancestry. It is the source of our most powerful ideas and experiences—such as strength, fight or flight, the concept of power, possibility, transcendence, awareness of self.[25] Jung also theorized that a neural substrate could contain a form of archetypal consciousness.[26] Imagine the molecular body alive with archetypal powers—what a mind blowing probability! Jung further states that "our evolutionary past provides a blueprint not only of our body but of our personalities, a blueprint carried in a so-called collective unconscious." [27]

Dr. Sharon G. Mijares in her studies in modern psychotherapy and ancient wisdom states that, "Memory is inherent in the DNA, genes, and cellular structure of the body/mind." Are these memories activated when, "the neural winds stream through the neural networks?"[28] In essence the collective kinetic blueprint within us is the *current* summation of the body's evolution from pre-human to animal to the current moment. You can extrapolate from there as to what it means if we carry—for instance—the experience of being a primate and living the use of tails, or the freedom of bi-pedal motion. These milestones along the continuum have left a kinetic path that we carry and can tap into—and which athletes engage. Gymnasts swinging from bar to bar, divers perfecting smooth entry into the water are tapping into skills needed for survival. Baseball pitchers

---

25 Jung, 1964, page 67. *Man and His Symbols.* (New York: Bantam Doubleday, 1968).

26 Jung, 1969, *On the Nature of the Psyche,* Collected works vol.8 Princeton: Bollingen Series.

27 Jung, *Collected Works.*

28 Mijares, 1995, 1997. Found on the internet, July 2012 at: http://www.seishindo. org/2009/04/04/rumi-jung-and-mythological-messages-from-the-body-mind/

are tapping into the muscle memory of the very first stone thrown at a predator. Swimmers tapping into the muscle memory of the first time a leg walked into the sea and experienced the power of a wave.

Modern body consciousness theory is replete with examples of the body/mind connection which Jung would applaud; after all, the body is our means of feeling, it houses our senses. Through it we experience the thrill and privilege of movement and action, life. And Walt Whitman's "body electric," might it, with its pulsing neural winds "whispering" learned-lessons from the past and "listening" neurons receiving or housing lessons, be advancing talent, skill? It would have to for the continuum to be dynamic not static. And the "body electric" in its base existence is anything *but* static.

There are multitudes of books on this subject regarding the burning of food in the metabolic mill to create the energy needed to support kinetic work, but can we make a connection between energy and the physical talent of an individual? Can we, "see talent as tangible as muscle and bone?" Daniel Coyle asks this question in his article on grooming a sports genius.[29] Does the energy of the universe that we have been musing about contribute and translate directly to something as ethereal and as difficult to achieve as talent? If so, wouldn't it seem that our very physical molecular make-up is then hard-wired, created, to play and *play well*? If we were only intended to exercise and move, then talent and getting better through practice and work wouldn't be a cellular by-product of them. Interestingly, we *are* created to play better! The more we execute skills the better we get at them. How? By the energy of neuron synapses firing over and over along the neuromuscular pathways. These pathways, encased in myelin, become the preferred pathways and the skill becomes easier, cleaner, more reliable and more predictable. How? The myelin sheath insulates the nerves more and more as the energy fires through. Like a good insulation on wires—none of the energy escapes.

When gymnasts and divers and bobsled drivers sit and do

---

29 "The *New York Times* Sports Magazine, *PLAY*" March 2007 article by Daniel Coyle.

visualizations of the tricks and course they must execute, the low level firing along the neuropathways actually thickens the pathway and makes it more likely to fire. So good habits are formed and also, the old adage of "bad habits are hard to break" is true. We are *created* to improve with practice. This is the key aspect of the collective kinetic blueprint—that we, as humans, across the time continuum of all societies and ages—advance ourselves with play. If we were only intended to move and utilize movement to achieve a task this wouldn't need to happen on a cellular level. But because we are created to evolve from task to talent—to skill—it shows that our Creator values play.

Physiologically we also pump out more "feel good" endorphins, as in a "runner's high" when we play *hard*—another sign that play is valued, rewarded, and intended to be a life-giving moment. These are all indications that we are indeed hard-wired to play— intended to play—and that one of the by-products of play matters is a better experience of life, and a happier self. *Play matters, so play as if it matters.* All humans are built to be able to experience these physiological benefits. We were created to enjoy the benefits of exercise and relaxation through the various forms and stages of play.

It is interesting here to note that this mechanism follows one of the basic laws of physics—conservation of energy. And the energy of human play follows the physical energy of matter. Energy in the metabolic mill enables the muscle to contract and fire. Energy in the neuromuscular pathways is protected and channeled by the myelin sheath. Kinetic energy in muscles is released and enables a track athlete to explode out of the starting blocks or hurl a javelin. The more one trains, the thicker the myelin sheath, the thicker the sheath, the better, clearer and cleaner the transmissions are, and the higher level of skill achieved!

Like the internet having a broader bandwidth that sends a sharper image faster—training leads to skilled athletes' whose neurological firings to the muscle fibers yield greater control and more precision. So teaching a skill properly is important to thicken the desired neuromuscular route. The firing of the nerve impulses comes from the exchange of ions on the cellular level where atoms are made of "dancing" energy strings. *Energy, energy, energy!*

And as the individual "improves" through play—thicker myelin strands, more highly skilled neuropathways, improved cardiovascular fitness develop (and these traits are genetically transferred to another)—and higher and more intricate levels are reached by the individual. As described by sport philosopher Joseph Espositio, "Sportive play engages the individual in the very act of becoming—a self transcendence to use Jean Paul Sartre's term."[30] The physical self becomes the vehicle for the transcendence to occur.

We see this in the Christ figure of the transfiguration in Jesus' transcendence of the biological self. Many cultures and religions use this similar idea of the gods being like humans and humans being like gods. We see this especially in sports, perhaps none more poignantly than in the Ancient Greeks and Romans. "The ancient Greek gods were anthropomorphic. As the French wit said, 'God created man in his own image and man returned the compliment.'" Greek sculpture portrayed the anthropomorphic gods as perfect physical specimens, to be both admired and emulated by their human worshipers."[31] The buildings and training grounds for physical education were replete with statues of the ancient gods. The athletes strove to honor them, be like them. The gods Hermes (for runners) and Hercules (for wrestling and boxing) were the two most significant gods of physical training. Artisans drawing form and capturing movement for sculptures and vases watched the athletes practice and immortalized their poses. The athletes worshiped the gods, performed for them, performed *to be like them.* They certainly strove to reach the heights of Olympia, to join the pantheon of gods if only for a fleeting moment at contests and games. And the people themselves, the fans of the city-states whose athlete won the precious olive leaf crowns sometimes had statues erected in *their* honor. Whole town walls were torn down to let the townsfolk see the procession of their returning victor. To

---

30   Morgan and Meier, 118.

31   Smith and Thompson, 34.

them there must have been a mere veil's width between mortal and immortal. The beauty of the "human form divine" beckoned athletes like a lover. Achievement of perfection was an invitation to god-ness. This pursuit of excellence urged athletes to seek the very heights of Mount Olympus, to literally come to the edge of where mortal flesh could go no further without an outpouring of the spirit—ecstasy—which will be discussed in a later chapter.

Collectively we share and benefit from this kinetic blueprint of energy that is surging through our beings. Again, we are *created* to improve with practice. This is the key aspect of the collective kinetic blueprint—that we, as humans, across the time continuum of all societies and ages—*advance ourselves with play.*

Probably the greatest testimony to this advancement is the Olympic Games. They are global, they demand the highest form of skill, they existed in various forms over thousands of years across many cultures, it is a stage for the making of heroes, where the fans are experiencing a collective unity and scintillating energy in the excitement of mass spectatorship and ritual, along the continuum of time.

How might this kinetic blueprint work? In identical mirror image twins such as the Winklevosses of the 2008 Beijing Olympic Games and Facebook fame, Tyler and Cameron in comparatively little preparatory time, rowed the straight pair to the Olympic finals. One rowed to the left, the other to the right—mirror images of each other. There are many twin combinations over the decades of the modern Olympic Games who excel because they are twins. They share the mass "collective" nature in their everyday existence. They are each part of the other—literally. I may share traits of genetic make-up with my older brother, but my genetic make-up didn't come from the same egg as his!

And through their playing—in this case rowing—the "closeness" they share in the physical realm and the "I know what he says or *does* before he does it" is a glimpse of what the collective *unconscious* is like, and what the collective kinetic blueprint is like. We move and can anticipate movement, because we are part of the collective fabric. There is a physical "signature" that becomes finer and finer, like good handwriting elevated through their play—rowing. They excel *because* of the kinetic blueprint. We all "carry it" and have been influenced by it and influence it—but twins may have the unique "team" mojo! Morgan and Meier state, "The body as object [of the individual] is transcended toward the body as pure activity; awareness of the other as co-player becomes transcended toward the awareness of coexistence of all players into a team."[32] Twins may be the ultimate example of what Morgan and Meier are referring to.

The collective unconscious leaves a kinetic footprint, a path, a structure; tell-tale signs of its existence and of its "having been there," *if* one knows what to look for—like reading a blue-print. The blue-print reflects what is. Such is the "strange country of the unreal that exalted place where we call upon the presences of the "essences" of things…play becomes symbol…human play is the symbolic action which puts us in the presence of the meaning of the world and of life."[33] We see these reflections in many ways, including but not limited to the superior skills we see "reflected" through thickening myelin sheaths, or heightened physiological interaction and ability reflected in exceptional interactions of "team-work." We feel the effects of "endorphins" that make us relaxed and feel peaceful and good—so we pursue them, try to harness them, master them, make them our own and ultimately leave a path of "how to get there"—for us and others to follow the next time. Humankind has collectively been doing these repetitive kinetic rituals since the first bi-pedals played tag in the primeval forest!

In the extraordinary 2012 History Channel documentary entitled, "How the Earth Made Man," one of the core themes was that we carry within us the collective experience of our evolutionary past—was stated by a distinctive collection of scientists across various disciplines and universities.[34] From the experience of déjà vu to

---

32 Morgan and Meier, 188.

33 Ibid., 108.

34 History Channel, 2012, *How the Earth Made Man.*

neuro-receptors that emit chemicals that relax us—universally—when we see images of the savannas, there are imprints in our minds carried through DNA that influence us today. One of the themes of the human condition changing over millions of years is that whatever we need to survive we take pleasure in. Play is pleasurable. Games are pleasurable and scientists are linking game playing and "choices" to gut feeling in roulette that pivot from gut feeling choices made in the dark of night when we were the hunted and needed instincts to survive and reaction times so short that they are not conscious—choices stemming from the collective unconscious. Eminent scientists are now recognizing that because of climate changes, Ice Ages, moving from sea to trees to savannas, that we are uniquely engineered to run in order to "out trot" predators and therefore today we enjoy running. We have biological ties, imprints, the kinetic imprint, to play, games, and sport.

Do we take advantage of this knowledge? Use it to our best ability? Sadly, it seems that there are many not taking advantage of the work it takes to play well! Attributes like focus and discipline are challenged routinely by a distracted generation tied to digital tablets and texting. In many ways, technology stills us. In the effort to make life easier and lift the burden of physical labor it decreases the physical. This trend toward stillness, stilling the pathways created to elate us, is a disconcerting dilemma running counter to fulfillment of destiny. And any coach or teacher who has been a practitioner for any length of time can speak of the apathy of many toward pursuing anything that demands discipline and focus and hard work. To deny the energy of play is to deny and impede the very energy of our existence. And that is why it is important, indeed essential, to delve into these concepts and understand them so as to inspire. Inspiration should be a by-product of our path, if we are leaving a path worth following. The collective unconscious and the trail of our kinetic footprint is a stamp on the fabric of the universe the end result of which is to advance us and to explain phenomena of play such as the breakthrough kinesis....

CHAPTER THREE

BREAKTHROUGH KINESIS [35]

In 1920 the Navy rowing team initiated an innovation in stroke style that caused them—and all other US men's eight crews until 1960—to win Olympic gold.[36] The nature of this occurrence goes beyond skill, effort, or training. Speculating on where that beyond might be and why such acts end up there is the focus of this paper. Relying primarily on the writings of the French philosopher M. Merleau-Ponty and his contemporary the eminent Swiss psychiatrist Carl Jung, this paper addresses a unique issue of movement change and presents the following theory regarding something I will call "breakthrough kinesis."[37] Using primarily the theories of Merleau-Ponty and Jung I will speculate on how intelligence and consciousness affect and create new and better movement.

Breakthrough kinesis occurs when a performance barrier, sometimes of mythic proportions, is finally overcome. While this unusual athletic advance may be grounded in several factors including better technology, invention, improved diet, superior coaching, and new equipment, it cannot be attributed entirely to these causes. A breakthrough kinesis has to do with a rebirth of hope, a new vision of human possibility. When a breakthrough takes place, when one athlete accomplishes the heroic act, other athletes are somehow

---

35 This chapter published with the permission of St. Martin's Press, New York, 2008. It is from the book, *The Wonder Crew: The Untold Story of a Coach, Navy Rowing, and Olympic Immortality*, by Susan Saint Sing.

36 "Navy Oarsmen Win By Half A Length," *New York Times*, 30 August 1920, S. p. 10.

37 Susan Saint Sing, "Breakthrough Kinesis," *Quest*, 2003, vol. 55. National Association for Physical Education in Higher Education.

emboldened and enabled. They too rush through the previously impenetrable gates.

Sport has been full of such barriers—the 4-minute mile, Babe Ruth's 60 home runs, the 7 foot high jump, ice-skating's quadruple jump, Ty Cobb's base hits, a sub-10 second 100 meter dash, the summiting of Everest without oxygen. As years passed and individual after individual fell short of these goals, the barriers became in some ways larger than life. "Out of reach," "can't ever be broken," "beyond human capability," "never seen in our lifetime," are descriptions often given to such mythic barriers. But strangely, when someone finally did surpass the mark, the barrier quickly lost its aura. The hero soon had company.

As old myths fall, of course, new myths take their place. Athletes are forever looking for the next great feat, the performance that resides just beyond what is humanly reasonable to expect—a perfect 10 in each event of All-Round gymnastics competition, a .400 season baseball average, a field goal kicker in football who places 80 yard kicks through the uprights every time, the archer who splits every arrow in a match. And when these speculative moments are someday reached, they too may be recognized instantly as the new mark, the better way of doing things.

These breakthrough feats, though possibly couched in invention or innovation, will advance the sport from that moment forward toward the next mythical realm. Differing from setting or surpassing a sport record as described and defined by noted historians Allen Guttmann and Richard Mandell, "breakthrough kinesis" represents a new—intangible—component added to a skill or event that thrusts the level of performance and aesthetics of the contest beyond the previously unattainable, beyond the scientific.[38] The idea of such an event as a breakthrough kinesis, can be intuited from the following

---

38   John Marshall Carter and Arnd Kruger, editors, *Ritual and Records: Sports Records and Quantification in Pre-Modern Societies* (Westport, Conn.: Greenwood Press, 1990), 3; Allen Guttmann, *From Ritual to Record: The Nature of Modern Sports* (New York: Columbia University Press, 1978), 50; Richard D. Mandell, *The Invention of the Sports Record*, Stadion II, (1976), 251.

passage in C.L.R. James' *Beyond a Boundary*: "The achievements of athletes in recent years which have so astonished the world are not as great as so many people imagine that they are. None of them is anywhere near the ultimate limits. By far the most important part of a great importance is played by the mind." He continues, "Long hours of training are not at all necessary." And, "the greatest performances will be produced by the 'poet, the artist, the philosopher.'"[39] Such a perception by the great cricketeer, James, turned social spokesman and philosopher is intriguing. His claims lead one to ponder other writings regarding the phenomenon of mind and performance, including Carl Jung and his theories of the collective unconscious. Is there a deeper "well" feeding the spring waters of great performances?

It seems that some philosophers imply that there must be something more than just aspects of athletic ability that can be attributed to hard work. Even those who explore the realms of the "inner athlete," are still looking primarily to the mind/body conscious abilities, in present time, to synthesize and execute. But what if time takes on a different role? What if the present is also heavily influenced by the past? What if the past is not lost back there, but it is with us, and the collective memories in that past consciousness are with us too? What if there is a collective body wisdom, inherited from all the past body movements of the human race and beyond, from the moment we learned to walk upright until now that is stored and transmitted in the collective unconscious as described by Jung? This would represent a collective kinetic intelligence in each one of us that is in the unconscious, that is passed from generation to generation and is greater than the single self embodiment knowledge of any one individual. Wouldn't that be something?

Historian and philosopher C.L.R. James, in *Beyond a Boundary*, muses about this phenomenon that I am wondering about when he writes that after Roger Bannister broke a mental barrier by running a sub four minute mile, it became easier and easier for others to surpass

---

39   C.L.R. James, *Beyond a Boundary* (Durham: Duke University Press, 1993; orig. 1963), 220-221.

that formerly unbeatable boundary. At times as many as three and four runners a day were doing it.[40] It was as if, through Bannister's run, humankind rose up and advanced. It was recognized, and accepted, yet remained perplexing. In Jungian terms, Bannister's run had influenced the collective unconscious of many, and the parameters of the sport of running were expanded.[41] How might this work, and what is the collective unconscious?

According to Jung, "In addition to our immediate consciousness, which is of a thoroughly personal nature and which we believe to be the only empirical psyche, there exists a *second* psychic system of a collective, universal and impersonal nature, that is identical in all individuals. This collective unconscious does not develop individually but is inherited. It consists of pre-existent forms, the archetypes, which can only become conscious secondarily and which give definite form to certain psyche contents."[42] The archetypes are images that arise from the unconscious and give it form. Jung discusses the use of the term archetype as stemming from the Greek, Roman, and early Church writings as the images that are found in various literary and mythological references.[43] Expression of the archetypes is in primordial, archaic forms or images such as those found in tribal lore, myth and fairy tales.[44] This is to say, cultures and societies, no matter how far dispersed on the planet in time or physical space, reflect images such as these in their verbal and written traditions that affect the race. Sporting traditions have had significant impact on societies and one would think that, by Jung's definition, would not be outside of the influences of the collective unconscious.

Sport culture and sporting behavior is a monumental component

---

40 James, 221.

41 Joseph Campbell, ed., *The Portable Jung* (New York: Penguin Books, 1982), 59. See also Carl J. Jung, *The Archetype and the Collective Unconscious*, The Collected Works of C. J. Jung, Bollington Series, (Princeton: Princeton University Press, 1956.) Jung first started writing on the collective unconscious in 1902.

42 Jung, *The Archetypes and the Collective Unconscious*, 43. Bollingen Series.

43 Ibid., 4.

44 Ibid., 5.

in most societies—it should therefore exhibit the archetypes that Jung describes. Can we then, as sport scientists, philosophers, and historians combine and synthesize across the discourse communities to fine-tune and decipher movement in these terms? Would Jung be appalled by such an attempt? In a recent phone interview, a psychiatrist told me that speculating on the possible influences of the collective unconscious on sport is "safe" and that Jung's concept of the collective unconscious has evolved historically and is dynamic. This is to say--the concept can be metaphorically "stretched" since it is not a static idea.[45]

As stated earlier, Jung's greatest contributions to the understanding of the psyche include the archetypes of the collective unconscious. Some such examples of archetypes are the images of rebirth, mother, trickster and hero. The images are re-created in settings or scenes of intense drama. For example, no need for a hero exists unless something is drastically wrong. For our purposes of understanding the "breakthrough kinesis," in particular, we must include Jung's further consideration that, "as personal complexes have their individual history, so do social complexes of an archetypal character. But while personal complexes never produce more than a personal bias, archetypes create myths, religions and philosophical ideas that influence and set their stamp on whole nations and epochs."[46]

Certainly the hero archetype is of interest to sport and has been the subject of many studies. Are the researchers unwittingly studying the public's response to the collective unconscious' archetypes? Sport psychologist, Janet Harris, in her work on American sporting heroes touches on the role of the athlete and the symbolic contribution to culture when talking about sports. "Talented athletes are clearly central components in the symbolic or expressive functioning of sport." Also, "Sports operate symbolically in ways similar to other

---

45   Phone conversation with Alex Weech, MD, psychiatrist and psychoanalyst 4/13/03. Dr. Weech was in Cincinnati, Ohio. Dr. Weech is a graduate of Princeton and Columbia Universities.

46   Carl Jung, *The Undiscovered Self,* The Collected Works of C. J. Jung, Bollingen Series, (Princeton: Princeton University Press, 1956. 118.

popular cultural performances."[47]

The symbolic component of sport is important and the movement intrinsic to sport is important. And looking at the aspects of intelligence and embodiment that facilitate movement as arising not just from skill, talent, and hard work, but also from the archetypes of the collective unconscious, to the conscious action executed by the athlete and witnessed by fans is largely unexplored. Examining and speculating on this link from the collective unconscious to the action of the present conscious state may constitute the beginning for understanding breakthrough kinesis.

Jung proposed that the collective unconscious is carried through the generations. Contemporary writer Leonard Shlain believes that Jung's idea of not coming into the world "as a *tabula rasa* devoid of any information, but rather as being born with the unconscious memories that embody the great events of our evolutionary development, extends Kant's proposal of *a priori* categories to include knowledge of archaic events."[48] What Shalin is saying is that Jung believed that symbols and myths (archetypes) like heroes, which have distinct and otherwise inexplicable commonalities found in all cultures, are universal because they are carried forward through time and space within the collective unconscious of the species.

Concomitantly, Merleau-Ponty speculates on the phenomenology of movement and also relates his early ideas and conceptions to myth and primordial images. Merleau-Ponty says, "mythical consciousness does indeed open on to a horizon of possible objectifications. Primitive man lives his myths against a sufficiently articulate perceptual background for the activities of daily life like fishing, hunting, and dealings with civilized people, to be possible. The myth itself, however diffuse, has an identifiable significance for primitive man, simply because it does form a world, that is, a whole in which each element has meaningful relations to the rest. It is true that

---

47   Janet Harris, *Athletes and the American Hero Dilemma*, (Champaign, IL: Human Kinetics, 1994) 2.

48   Leonard Shlain, *Art and Physics* (New York: Harper Collins, 1991), 412.

mythical consciousness is not a consciousness of any thing. That is to say that subjectively it is a flux, that it does not become static and thus does not know itself."[49]

Being in a state of flux, and in a state of not knowing itself is interesting. What does it mean to know itself or not know itself? Does Merleau-Ponty mean one does not recognize aspects of the self inside the self because the conscious and the unconscious do not readily communicate? Or does the not knowing, become known, thus recognized, when an unconscious phenomenon breaks out and skids across the stage of consciousness in such astounding presence and to such thundering applause that it instantly brings the conscious global audience to its feet—as if jumping out of their theater seats? Such would be an explanation for breakthrough kinesis. Jung encourages these moments stating that "by distilling the experience of one's life, one affirms that the survival of our civilization may well depend upon closing the widening gulf between the conscious and unconscious aspects of the human psyche."[50]

Philosopher Michael Novak distills the power of athletic experience in the revelatory moments of perfect form.[51] Novak looks at these psychically enhanced performances, if you will, in sport and likens them to being or coming from or belonging to another plane (the spiritual, perhaps, in Novak's understanding). But Novak's description I believe also captures the essence of a "breakthrough kinesis" in the following passage: "Tens of thousands of passes are thrown every year, thousands of games are played in grammar schools, high schools, colleges, and professional stadia; all the routines are thoroughly known. Occasionally, however, often enough to stir the heart, a player or a team executes a play so beautifully, achieves such classic perfection, that it is as though they cease for a moment to be pedestrian and leap into a realm of precision as lovely as a statue of Praxiteles. Athletic achievement, like the achievements of

---

49 M. Merleau-Ponty, *Phenomenology of Perception*, translated from the French by Colin Smith (London: Routledge and Kegan Paul, 1962), 292.

50 Jung, *The Undiscovered Self*,

51 Michael Novak, *The Joy of Sports* (New York: Basic Books, 1976), 5.

the heroes and the gods of Greece, is the momentary attainment of perfect form—as though there were, hidden away from mortal eyes, a perfect way to execute a play, and suddenly a player or a team has found it and sneaked a demonstration down to earth. A great play is a revelation. The curtains of ordinary life part, and perfection flashes for an instant before the eye."[52]

To this reader, the phrase "hidden away from mortal eyes, a perfect way" is the key to Novak's explanation. Where is the "perfect way" "hidden," yet available to the extent that we witness it enough times that people recognize it, philosophers think about, writers elaborate on it and athletes occasionally achieve it? Does it lie in Merleau-Ponty's realm of unrecognized unconsciousness coming to know itself in the conscious act? I think one must answer that it lies within the mind/body experience in a rare yet certain intersection of space, planes, consciousness, movement, and moment. I think that the element of "moment" or "timing" is unique to breakthrough kinesis because it places the action in a unique reference to all other actions past and future. It is THIS action—right now—that is the first and therefore the unique breakthrough and it came forth due to a paradigm shift in the collective unconscious of body knowledge.

Speculating within the framework of Jung again with his idea of synchronicity, Jung believed that all human events interweave on a plane to which we are not consciously privy, so that in addition to prosaic cause and effect, human events are joined in a higher dimension by meaning. What is the higher level of meaning? Could it be that a collective "body knowledge" of all the bodies who have moved and lived and the collective—collected—wisdom of those experiences? The sum total would be an enormous experience of wealth and wisdom of physical perception that it could, and speculatively would, supersede any one single embodiment. The perception of Roger Bannister's accomplishment by James was that many people went with Bannister, through this barrier. Once the gate was open the log jam cleared, because the wave rising from

---

52   Ibid.

the collective unconscious of embodiment took many single bodies with it. We are created and set up to see the individual effort, but James articulated the synchronicity of the phenomenon as a mental barrier that many people passed through once it was broken. This is to say that many people almost immediately shared the idea or the energy or at least the benefit of Bannister's accomplishment. It seems that Jung's idea of a collective unconscious that could connect and influence so many athletes makes sense. Almost as if there was a mass embodiment—unique to that brief moment in time for that event—that took place. Like a fold or an intersection in planes or energy fields of the collective unconsciousness—something is made conscious to all, that is remarkable, that is irrefutable, that exists; and then the wave disseminates back to the individual one-on-one embodiment experience, which is the individual ego's normal relational stance to the world. A breakthrough kinesis has occurred.

Examining the concept of what constitutes a breakthrough kinesis, one might argue that while the issue of Bannister is clear enough, what about something like Fosbury's "Flop" in the 1968 Mexico Olympics that won gold and turned the world of high-jumping literally upside down?[53] Is that a breakthrough or just an invention? I would say that breaking the mythical 7 foot high-jump barrier was a breakthrough kinesis and that the "flop" aided humankind in vaulting beyond that barrier. A breakthrough kinesis does not conflict with the idea of invention but enhances it. A breakthrough kinesis can come out of the blue, or it can be embedded in what is seen as an invention that someone clearly has been imagining or pondering. Breakthrough kinesis would not be in conflict with chemist and social scientist, Michael Polyani's, concerns that even the most remarkable inventions

---

53 Dick Fosbury's breakthrough when he altered modern day high jumping forever with his now famous "Fosbury Flop" in the 1968 Olympics would be an example of a breakthrough kinesis. (The "Fosbury flop is a method of high jumping where the athlete clears the bar with the back toward the bar instead of the face and stomach toward the bar.) See also "Keino Breaks Olympic Record in 1500-meter Run, With Ryan of the U.S. Second: U.S. Wins 3 Golds Medals in Relays-Fosbury Takes High Jump Record at 7-4 ½ inches" by Neil Amdur. *New York Times*, 21 October 1968, Lt. p. 60.

can become common place.[54]

There are many inventions, even inventions that work well, that do not influence and cause change on a global scale and never become common place. Torvel and Dean e.g., when they skated to *Bolero* and won the gold medal in ice-dance at Lake Placid in the 1980 Olympics invented the notion of lying on the ice for 18 seconds while the music played, creating a dramatic backdrop of suspense. They stayed on the ice for 18 seconds before they began to skate. The rules state that the timing of the performance does not begin until the "skating" begins. Obviously they invented a very dramatic and effective dance element. After all it won the gold medal.[55] However, unlike the Fosbury Flop that brought an about-face, literally throughout the high-jumping world, Torvel and Dean's invention did not touch any mythical barrier and is today recognized as a beautiful anomaly. In short, it did not breathe life into the sport by carrying skating, as a whole, to a new or sustained level. In contrast, when the Navy Admirals surpassed *Britannia* in the 1920 Olympic rowing event, their win began an unprecedented forty year winning streak of Olympic gold in the men's eights. American rowing "beat" its own origins by surpassing Britain on that day—and all that the British sporting traditions and rivalries entailed to the American athlete of that era. It was akin to the mythical slaying of Goliath. A breakthrough kinesis can include invention, technique, innovation, or be occasioned by it. Yet it is also something more.

A breakthrough kinesis is graced with the mythical. "Breakthrough kinesis" represents a new component added to a skill or event that advances the level of performance and aesthetics of the contest. What is the component? If it isn't just the imagination integrating Merleau-Ponty's pool of tacit knowledge, and it isn't just an attribute such as innovation or invention—what is it? To answer that question by way of example, all athletes and coaches would agree

---

54 Michael Polanyi and Harry Prosch, *Meaning*, (Chicago and London: The University of Chicago Press, 1975), 96-97.

55 Allen Guttmann, *The Olympics*, (Urbana and Chicago: University of Illinois Press, 1994), 157.

that we advance physiologically by plateaus. We reach plateaus, we stay there awhile and then we advance, upwards to the next level, the next plateau. The training curve is rarely a straight line or a symmetrical curve, rather, it looks more like steps. A breakthrough kinesis is such an advancement. The collective unconscious moves the mind/body to another level in a leap forward where it remains for a time before another breakthrough. This leap is in the realm of intangible that stumps science because it cannot be reduced to any "thing." It has, is, and forever retains, the element of the mythical. And, I have speculated that the collective unconscious helps to explain the mythical. For if we do carry within ourselves a collective memory of the experiences from all those who have lived before us to the very beginnings of our origins, we carry, and in fact are those origins.[56] Extending presumably, earlier than eyes and the ability to integrate subsidiaries and concepts of Polyani and Merleau-Ponty, to the essence of the mythical exchange in Michelangelo's "Touch." Be it God or a god or an unnamed energy that created what became who we are—the collective unconscious has its beginnings in that primordial era which is why its images are based in the fear of fire, the fear of falling, and the like. They are primeval. Our ability to learn, and the way in which we learn and set forth our experiences has a much greater potential than the single lifetime of collective subsidiaries for instance, when we include the gamut of possibilities of the collective unconscious. We then include all the time and space in which human consciousness and the forming of human consciousness has had through the ages, to form the background "screen" on which to perceive and view, in example, the idea of subsidiaries. A background

---

56 There are numerous mythological sayings and legends that preserve and promote this common idea through many civilizations. A Celtic stone from 400, A.D. I once visited has a Rune inscription that says "god within, god without, how can I ever be in doubt, I am the sower and the sown, god's self unfolding and god's own." Also the Christian myth of: "we are within God, as we are within ourselves, and within one another" is a similar idea of being one with the beginning, and one every current person, as well as our single self, through spiritual connection, simultaneously in the Body of Christ. The Alpha and the Omega of Christian belief symbolically represents the continuum of the beginning and the end being as one experience.

including the entirety of human experience which our present self at times taps into and integrates into a current day occurrence.

I think Merleau-Ponty expresses, touches on the essence of these occurrences this way: "We need to say merely that the phenomenal layer is literally pre-logical and will always remain so."[57] Natural and primordial space is not geometrical space, nor, correspondingly, is the unity of experience guaranteed by any universal thinker arraying its contents before me and ensuring that I possess complete knowledge of, and exercise complete power over it.[58] And stepping further into these phenomenal layers of Merleau-Ponty, the quantum physicist Frijof Capra might interpret these layers as folds of energy previously unseen as a "something," as a presence that "warps" the time and space around the occurrence in such a way as to "map" the incidence of the action: a breakthrough kinesis.[59]

In conclusion, though Jung is not here to dispel my errors or concerns I feel it is safe to at least theorize or ponder these ideas that there is a collective unconscious; and it contributes and, in fact, may create the phenomenon I recognize as breakthrough kinesis and that sports figures, heroes have been the recipients of that symbolic, mythical wreath from the unconscious more often than not. People seek heroes, they seek the times of "breakthrough kinesis"; as George Santayana says in the 1800s, "...only the sublime is worth while, everything else is held up to it."[60]

I realize that these thoughts ask one to stretch the known relationship of mind/body embodiment to form a cohesive past, present, and future through the collective unconscious that leaves us all waiting on the edge of our collective kinetic intelligence seat, waiting for the next moment of "breakthrough kinesis" that informs

---

57 Merleau-Ponty, *Phenomenology*, 274.

58 Ibid., 294.

59 The writings of Merleau-Ponty inspired many physicists to theorize in quantum physics. Some writings in this subject area are: *Fritjof Capra* and David Stendl-Rast, *Belonging to the Universe*. See also Fritjof Capra, *The Tao of Physics*, 136.

60 George Santayana "Philosophy on the Bleachers," Harvard Monthly XVIII (July 1894), 184.

us with our recognition of its greatness—that we have once again advanced. The idea stretches the imagination and in the words of Julien Offray de la Mettrie asks us to, "Break the chain of your prejudices, arm yourselves with the torch of experience, and you will render to nature the honor she deserves, instead of inferring anything to her disadvantage, from the ignorance in which she has left you."[61]

---

61 Eugene Freeman, editor, *Man A Machine and The Natural History of the Soul*—Julien Offray de la Mettrie (Chicago: Open Court Publishing Co., 1912), 82.

CHAPTER FOUR

AGON AND
THE HERO ATHLETE

When I was speaking at a Vatican conference in Rome, I was asked a question that got me thinking about pain and athletes. Having suffered a broken neck and back myself in a gymnastics accident and having spent ten years in a pain control center—while still searching for another way to *still* be an athlete—I decided to take up the invitation and challenge of an esteemed colleague and examine further the question of athletes and pain. So, in this chapter I will attempt to examine why athletes expect and embrace pain, and what it is that they find in pain that perhaps can expand or illuminate a more positive side to this seeming self-flagellation. If we can pin-point patterns, then we can, as educators and coaches gain useful information for the whole. For as educators, coaches, or athletes ourselves, if we can understand *why* an athlete pursues these extremes and accepts them as normal—even necessary—to advance, then we have an obligation to explore with athletes in order to name and understand the means toward this pursuit of excellence. Toward that end, this chapter is divided into four parts: (1) the underlying (at times unconscious) collective thrust of the hero athlete, leading to (2) the conscious athletic pursuit which includes the struggle of pain of several types, (3) the edge, which leads to (4) that which is beyond the edge—the mystical, spiritual experience that some athletes achieve through *agon.*

In the ancient world of Homer and Odysseus, *agon* is the conflict within and without in which a person is rated and judged in their pursuit of excellence. More than just competition and certainly more than our English word of agony, *agon* is a state of embodiment. Odysseus's wife was *Arête*, which translated loosely means beauty, but in a larger sense means—strength in beauty—effectiveness. These legends came to depict qualities of life to strive toward. Virtues. To the ancient Greeks these two concepts of *agon* and *arête* were statements of character. It is the heroic virtue St. Paul speaks of when he says, "I have fought the good fight, I have finished the race, I have kept the faith" in Second Timothy. Athletes strove through *agon* to achieve *arête*. In the ideal, they pursued excellence in mind/body/spirit. Athletes were to be balanced and schooled in song, poetry, dance, strength of character as well as physical strength. It is my hope to examine this embodied virtue of *agon* and its components—such as the inevitable pain of struggle—in this chapter. It has been depicted by the masters throughout the ages in illuminating forms of art, film, poetry, literature, and sculpture. *Agon* can be terribly beautiful as in R.T. McKenzie's 4 famous masks of facial emotion in a runner and Michelangelo's stone "Prisoners" struggling to free themselves. *Agon* and its components is by nature inspiring and is always complex.

At this point, I think it is important to mention that physical pain can involve suffering. And for the sake of this discourse I am generally applying my thoughts to physical pain and suffering, more so than emotional suffering—such as disappointment and loss though they are clearly acknowleged as part of the struggle.

THE HERO ATHLETE

Hero in Greek mythology is the Greek goddess pursued by Leander who swims across the Hellespont, in pursuit of ecstasy and love, who tries every night to cross and is eventually lost in a storm. Leander is a swimmer, an athlete—thus, the first Hero myth is of an athlete.

The eminent psychoanalyst, Carl Jung, believes that the collective unconscious links us in a continuum to primordial archetypal images that we have an imprint of from a beginning that we share within us and from which these myths arise across all cultures and times. He lists theses archetypes that recur from the collective unconscious of humankind; some of these archetypes are: "mother," "trickster," "wise-man," "hero." Jung takes these archetypes and enlarges them from the individual to the collective human plane. He then terms existence and relationships as collective experiences that are structured in part by unconscious archetypes. If an athlete is one who is seeking the external, the physical limits of performance, of self, then finding the internal boundaries, the journey within, is as equal a challenge. Once an athlete commits to excel externally through running the fastest, or jumping the highest, etc., the internal struggle to achieve these feats becomes part of the means.

I believe that one of the unconscious links is the tendency in human nature to explore boundaries. Sigmund Freud, master and originator of the science of the unconscious, states that we as developing humans need boundaries; indeed, we are comforted once we know where the boundaries are because they help define our limits, and define who we are in our existence and relationships.[62]

While each individual's experience of the boundary, tolerance of the boundary, perception of the boundary, may be unique, the fact that a boundary exists for us to look for is the critical element. Specific to the athlete, part of what I have termed elsewhere a kinetic blueprint within the collective unconscious is the need to know and "locate" boundaries, the edge that is us, that defines us physically as well.[63] Kinetically we use our handedness and footedness to frame this blueprint of physical self. How fast we can ride a bike can be one athlete's self definition.

The first hero myth of Leander involved an athlete with pain. When the wind blew the light out guiding Leander, an athlete strong

---

62 Sigmund Freud, *Collected Works*. Freud's concept of boundaries for and within the self was written about extensively throughout his lifetime as he continued to elaborate and develop his ideas of self.

63 Susan Saint Sing, "Breakthrough Kinesis," *Quest*, 2003, vol. 55. National Association for Physical Education in Higher Education.

enough to swim night after night across the Hellespont, he drowned pursuing his love. This archetype of the Hero is part of the collective unconscious of humankind artfully described by Jung. We in turn, as athletes, seek to and in fact are driven to unite with that archetype to capture part of the hero in ourselves and so we flirt with that edge between the mortal and the divine, the ordinary love and the heroic that swims night after night… in order to not be common. On one of the edges is the common self, the mundane, on the other side is greatness, the hero, and so we flirt with that line. We approach it, we touch it, we achieve it, we surpass it and we feel we have grown and gone beyond self… we have become a part of something greater, beyond the mortal. We have reached the edge of mortality and the boundary of self's limit, and in reaching that edge we seek to break through to a higher kinetic plane—a movement I call breakthrough kinesis.

The controversial, recently de-medaled, Lance Armstrong, as one example of an elite athlete who has suffered through self-inflicted physical pain and the involuntary pain of brain and testicular cancer, talks about this edge and the exploration like this: "There is no reason to attempt such a feat of idiocy, other than the fact that some people, which is to say some people like me, have a need to search the depths of their stamina for self-definition. (I'm the guy who can take it.) It's a contest in purposeless suffering. But for reasons of my own, I think it may be the most gallant athletic endeavor in the world. To me, of course, it's about living."[64]

In the myth of the hero athlete to go to the "edge" one must endure pain. To achieve is to endure pain—it is a given.

If we can understand *what happens when* true athletes, elite athletes, enter into these extreme struggles, we can help them achieve their goals as well as get a glimpse into a world few of us might ever be willing to enter wholly into. It does not do much good to know what an individual does if it isn't applicable to a larger group. So

---

64   Lance Armstrong, *It's not about the bike, My Journey back to Life*. (New York: Berkley Publishers, 2001) 212-213.

then, if we can find a link to "athlete" that places the individual into the greater whole of the collective psyche, we have something more universal—more helpful because it is more applicable to the general and not isolated to the outlier or the unique. Then we as educators and coaches or maybe athletes can more readily utilize the process to guide others.

Additionally, one might ask, what about a baseball player or bowler, since he or she does not endure pain the same way as an endurance athlete might? Are they not part of the hero athlete archetype? Archetypes are representative of energies in the collective unconscious that influence; they are not like photographs with distinct images but more like impressionist paintings that allow the mind to fill in the blanks. They are not still ponds, but more like bubbling springs that seep up and find outlets for expression. And the fact that the myth blankets sports and athletes *in general* is characteristic of the archetypes. How many times have we seen a baseball player who is hit with a ball told to "walk it [the hurt] off" or "play through the pain?" The baseball player might not endure the training of a Lance Armstrong, but since the myth is greater than the individual, the expectation people have is that an, or any, athlete will endure pain because we are influenced by the hero archetype.

PAIN

Michael McNamee, in his, "Suffering in and for Sport," asks two questions that stuck in my mind: "What ends are served by suffering in and for sport?" And "What qualities attend the suffering?"[65] These two questions kept me awake at night until I could find an answer, at least a partial and perhaps minimal answer. As a past national team athlete and one who suffered, both voluntarily for the sake of winning, and involuntarily in an accident that forced me into a pain

---

65 Loland, S.; Skirstad, B; Waddington, I. (eds.). *Pain and Injury in Sport Sport: Social and Ethical Analysis.* (London: Routledge, 2006) "Suffering In and for Sport: Some Philosophical Remarks on a Painful Emotion" Chapter 14 by Michael McNamee, 242-243.

control clinic for a decade, I have been asked from time to time to elaborate on my experiences of pain and suffering. At a conference I was asked about what steps I took that others might follow in order to reach an understanding, meager as it may be, of the labyrinth of pain and what end it served. Toward that end I think there are three types of pain athletes are subjected to: voluntary, such as in training; involuntary, such as in injury; and cognitive, both voluntary and involuntary, such as in coaching when a coach consciously plans and judges the pain allotted in the discipline of that training for another, or involuntarily sets goals that incidentally involves pain.

So, why pain? As I've mentioned above, athletes search for the edges, the extremes of mortality which are ecstasy on one hand and pain (unto death at times) on the other. We reach ecstasy and joy often by going through pain to get there and so the two are intertwined. With the pain often lasting longer than the joy, pain is accepted as part of the quest for joy. The literature and poetry of the Romantic Period have portrayed and alluded to this coincidence of seeming opposites as part of humanity's struggle, such as these few lines from John Keats "Ode to a Nightingale":

Now more than ever seems it rich to die,
To cease upon the midnight with no pain,
While thou art pouring forth thy soul abroad
In such an ecstasy! [66]

It is only a drive as strong as love that would keep someone in the hunt, in the pursuit—passion is a driving force and a common thread throughout an athlete's pursuit—she or he *loves* their sport. Pain then, self-inflicted becomes more palatable, and an involuntary injury or sickness more despised because it takes them away from that which they love. Most participate knowing that even death can occur in their pursuit.

---

66   Keats, John. "Ode to a Nightingale."

In Evelyn Underhill's book, *Mysticism*, the author writes, "life as we know it has the character of a purposeful striving…. Some form of feeling—interest, desire, fear, appetite—must supply the motive power. …The heart has its reasons which the mind knows not of, it is a matter of experience that in our moments of deep emotion, transitory though they may be, we plunge deeper into the reality of things than we can hope to do in hours of the most brilliant argument. At the touch of passion doors fly open which logic has battered in vain: for passion rouses to activity not merely the mind, but the whole vitality of man."[67] Which is in essence what Armstong describes in a similar vein but different rhetoric.

Moreover, Underhill, when talking about mysticism, speaks of it as "essentially the movement of the heart seeking to transcend the limitations of the individual."[68] Underhill goes on to say that mysticism is the "giving" and super-sensual is the wanting "to get" something of these heightened experiences. I would humbly like to try and loosely knit these profound concepts into the athlete's purpose of striving to the point of pain to get personal gain—winning perhaps—but also the giving of self, the literal mortal self toward that end. And while not being bold enough to compare the athlete's striving to the heights and intricacies of spiritual mysticism, there are similarities, that make me wonder whether it is the same drive in us, namely to explore and seek the edges and barriers of ourselves to thereby get a view of what is beyond? It is one of the deepest questions of humankind: What are we a part of and in what capacity does our existence participate in this greater whole?

For the true athlete hero, a medal is not the goal, but like the lone sculler on a lake in the morning fog or a lone runner, he or she trains and suffers for the shear pursuit of *becoming*, or at least seeming to become something more and for a few seconds perhaps, does become *something greater than the self was a few seconds before*. Faster, or stronger…he or she has changed, and

---

67 *Mysticism: A study in the Nature and Development of Man's Spiritual Consciousness*, Evelyn Underhill, 48.

68 Ibid.

it took going to the edge to evoke that change and it is worth it because of the ecstasy that follows.

THE EDGE

We have countless books on ecstasy, but it is the counterpoint—physical pain and suffering—that this chapter addresses. It is the same pursuit, but along the opposing direction of a circle that comes all the way around through great pain to ecstasy again. Joseph Campbell calls it the up and down of life which are two turns of the same key, the totality of the revelation of life.[69] And then one is never "normal," again, never common because of the experience of having achieved—even momentarily—the goal of peeking across the edge, from the edge of human physicality to the beyond. It is the Beyond that is the goal and what makes the pain worth the struggle. And we, like Leander the athlete of love, die in pursuit of being one with Hero, who then seeks to join the struggle and succumbs with the pursuer in something like Keats' death/ecstasy dynamic.

These archetypal drives would not count pain as a great sacrifice. Pain becomes expected and part of the necessary path to achieve the goal, so it is sacrificial as well as directive. The pain becomes the path and therefore is sought after, endemic to the athlete's pursuit. I think there are perhaps three types of pain athletes are subjected to: voluntary such as in the athlete driving themselves training, involuntary such as in injury, and cognitive, such as in coaching when a coach consciously plans and judges the pain allotted in the discipline of the training and the athlete willingly complies.

Leander expected pain on that dark stormy night as much as he expected victory and attainment. Leander's failure in the pursuit of love, while painful, is at least more palatable in that it occurred in pursuit of something higher. Death comes naturally, and an athlete

---

69   Joseph Campbell, *The Hero with a Thousand Faces*, (The Bollingen Series xviii, CA: New World Library) 2008, page 22. This is from the third edition of the Bollingen Series of the collected works of Joseph Campbell. His *The Hero with a Thousand Faces* was originally published in 1949.

toys with that edge of life and death and the Beyond of limits in order to conquer death for a moment and join the immortal, the kinetic pantheon.

As Joseph Campbell describes in his book, *Hero of a Thousand Faces*, "the point is not that such-and-such was done on earth; the point is that before such-and-such could be done on earth, this other, more important, primary thing had to be brought to pass...."[70]

As in the myth of Leander and the goddess Hero, there is the goal and the effort united and accomplished through suffering, and even the repeated suffering of Leander's nightly swims. It would seem that in the human condition goal and suffering are conjoined. In one graph of the Hero-Journey the edge could be referred to as the Threshold to Transformation, where the hero suffers tests, usually physical tests before crossing the edge, this threshold to what?[71] The physical edge of mortal being is immortality or non-existence, the edge of physical if it be immortality includes then, the spiritual. All can be encompassed across cultures as myth.

As in the Monomyth of a James Joyce and a Joseph Campbell, the hero crosses all societies, as does play. Sociologists tell us that all cultures play and through play we create our sports heroes, propagating the hero athlete for our period of time on the continuum and moving the myth into the next generation of the collective unconscious that will benefit from our advances of the kinetic blueprint we are unifying, polishing, amalgamating—hopefully toward a higher plane.[72] The athlete, like the hero goes through the Abyss of death through relentless training and pain to reach the rebirth of the new self and after this transformation: "the elixir, knowledge or blessing that the hero acquired in the adventure can now be put to use in the everyday world. Often it has a restorative or healing function,

---

70   Ibid.

71   Carl G. Jung, *Man and his Symbols* (New York: Bantam Doubleday Dell Publishing, 1968).

72   Ehrenreich, *Dancing in the Streets* (New York: Henry Holt Publishing, Metropolitan Books, 2006).

but it also serves to define the heroes' role in society."[73] One need only look at the price tag of any recent Olympic game to know the athlete-heroes' role in society and the myriad stories of pain that were endured to reach that podium. And like the heroes of ancient Greece, we listen to Olympians tell their stories of adventure as any hero does who "returns from this mysterious adventure with the power to bestow boons on his fellow man."[74] In short, we as fans, intuitively want to know and understand and even seek what is learned there by the individual, what was encountered there on those edges/thresholds of transformation because the individual experience is intended for the betterment of the whole that is symbolic of the possible. Furthermore, sport psychologist Janet Harris, in her study of American sport states the essential role sport heroes play as "central components in the symbolic or expressive functioning of sport."[75] Ed Smith in discussing master storyteller Simon Barne's book *The Meaning of Sport* explores how myth, "is central to the whole business of sport and how sport taps into the essential stories of human nature... the sportsmen are the mythic heroes."[76] Heroes and the pain-journey they take are intrinsic to and aid the very function of sport and aid societies' collective need to engage in myth.

Here lies the realm, for some who have passed along this route, of those who become the wisdom figures for others because of their sojourn. They have been transformed, not only in physical appearance or physiological conditioning, but in the enlightened, higher state of the mind/body/soul trinity. Michael Novak, in his treatise on sport, myth and religion, *The Joy of Sports*, unabashedly connects sport to liturgy, a natural religion, packed by myths, not the least being his interpretation of the seven seals of sport: sacred time, sacred space,

---

73 Found on the Internet at http://orias.berkeley.edu/hero/JourneyStages.pdf, January 2010.

74 Found on the Internet at http://orias.berkeley.edu/hero/JourneyStages.pdf, January 2010.

75 Janet Harris, *Athletes and the American Hero Dilemma*. (Champaign IL: Human Kinetics 1994).

76 "The Spectator," 18 November 2006, 53.

bond of brothers, rooting, agon, competing, and self-discovery.[77] Wouldn't most, if not all, of these be common in a spiritual journey or experience? St. Paul speaks clearly to the parallels of sport and spirituality; and others, like Michael Novak, might see this form of "map making" or "mystical way" as it corresponds to the mystical way in Christianity, as the very human passion we go through as athletes. Taken all as a whole, there is a transcendence from physical to spiritual that is "woven" into the "character" or the nature of the evolving person through this flowing stream of mind/body/soul that is no longer individual elements of mind, body, soul—but is perhaps now, as then, *arête* (the culmination of excellence, in physical and intellectual power and strength which the ancients strived for) made manifest.

All of this theorizing is easily said on paper, but what of the great athletes who have sought to pursue the extremes and have gone through the *unwanted, uninvited* pain of injury which thrusts pain upon them as opposed to the willing entry into the necessary pain of training? Perhaps these athletes should be seen to have experienced "the Dark Night of the Soul." The Garden of Gethsemane that many athletes go through when severe disappointment or injury brings them across the "Hellespont" of their passion—does this advance us too? Or is it a waste?

Collective wisdom would tell us that you don't get far in life without encountering the darkness, and you don't get far in athletics without encountering pain. Pain can include so many components, a few being: the daily grind of the training regimen, injury, competing; but these, when embraced in love, can be piercing moments of stigmatic unity of the physical and the spiritual at last inextricably met, if only in the memory of the achiever. Hope can be born in such moments! Hope—faith—to recover, to be able to achieve, to believe the unattainable goal is attainable, is part of the journey. Hope *is* part of the spiritual pantheon. As Novak says, "to fights one's way through opposition to do what one wills to do,

---

77   Novak, *The Joy of Sports.*

against odds, against probabilities–these are to practice a very high art, to achieve a few moments of beauty that will delight the memory of those who watched, or listened, or read, for all their lives. What we mean by "[sports] legend" is what we mean by "art": the reaching of a form, a perfection, which ordinarily the flesh masks, a form eternal in its beauty. It is as though muscle and nerves and spirit and comrades were working together as flawlessly as God once imagined human beings might."[78]

That we have in our collective unconscious this kinetic blueprint of athlete/hero, is part of our social, anthropological self, and the athlete, while perhaps more attuned to this, is but a part of the mature surface expression—that is to say, consciousness, of the developing ego strengths, otherwise known as maturity. Children avoid pain, maturity brings the understanding that pain can mean growth, and accompany growth, and therefore is not avoided but pursued.

A willingness to suffer pain, indeed the essential acceptance of suffering, is key to the underlying hero archetype. An athlete would need to endure suffering in order to be a hero, and a hero must endure suffering and pass initiations and rites of passage involving athletic qualities in order to be a hero. There is a cyclical intertwining of these crucial events. To reiterate, suffering is a component of physical pain, though certainly suffering can be of a mental, emotional nature too that has no physical origin.

As stated, the hero archetype includes initiation or rite of passage that is usually physical such as winning a race or wrestling, which acts as a qualifier.[79] Typically with these passages there is a proof of strength that the hero must exhibit and then ultimately the hero must struggle with forces that try to destroy it or hold it back; the hero usually is assisted by tutelage (coaching), and ultimately dies or sacrifices self for the betterment of the whole. Cycling uses this as a

---

78   Novak, *The Joy of Sports*, 16-17.

79   Jung, *Man and His Symbols* (New York: Bantam Doubleday Dell Publishing, 1968). p 105.

tactic literally to save and then advance one rider and figuratively to thrust the pantheon of sport heroes both ancient and modern before civilization's waiting face to insure and witness, if nothing else, hope, achievement, even virtue at sport's best.

Jung defines heroes thus: These godlike figures are in fact symbolic representatives of the whole psyche, the larger and more comprehensive identity that supplies the strength that the personal ego lacks. Their special role suggests that the essential function of the heroic myth is the development of the individual's ego-consciousness—his awareness of his own strengths and weaknesses—in a manner that will equip him for the arduous tasks with which life confronts him.[80]

Certainly one of the most arduous tasks in life is to comprehend the meaning of pain and suffering, and mortality. Sometimes, entering into the mystical brings the mortal to the edge of what is beyond. Athletes are defining this for themselves, and thus for others, everyday. Is that why we cheer them as fans? Is that why we, as observers are mystically in a vicarious union with their feats? In their pain and in their triumph over and through it? Because they are making our way, too; through the labyrinth of daily struggle we hero-ize them for pushing the envelope and bumping up against the edge—expanding it for us, too?

If so, and if such qualities attributed to pain suffering are better understood and the collective whole can see these distinguishable areas of pain, perhaps it fills a void in the literature so that as sport philosophers and coaches and trainers and athletes we deepen our understanding of the human condition and perhaps guide "novices" as well as appreciate "masters" through the rite of passage they are mapping for others, the mystical road toward the next breakthrough kinesis.[81] Sport, then, serves the end of suffering toward excellence, toward betterment, toward unity and wholeness. However, this

---

80 Jung, *Man and His Symbols*, 101.

81 Susan Saint Sing, "Breakthrough Kinesis," Quest, 2003, vol. 55. National Association for Physical Education in Higher Education.

chapter does acknowledge that pain and suffering can also unmake worlds and leave shattered dreams and at times, shattered individuals. No one passes through a labyrinth easily, and it is those who have gotten through who testify to the positive attributes of suffering, sadly, there are personal tragedies.

Jeffrey P. Fry in his objective study of pain and how individuals perceive, justify, and interpret it as spiritual, beneficial, or destructive finds that there is "cumulative weight" to the testimonies of "positive appraisals of pain and suffering in sport."[82] This cumulative weight is what this paper supports—that there is something ethereal going on in suffering that athletes and coaches need to explore and tap into the positive aspects of. Pain and suffering have both negatives and positives. Analyzing and synthesizing ideas across various disciplines can only aid athletes and coaches in tapping into the positives. One need only see the recent antiapartheid film, *Invictus*, about the role of rugby in helping to unite South Africa after Apartheid to appreciate the larger call of the athlete's kinetic footprint in making a path worth following....

---

82   S. Loland; B. Skirstad; I. Waddington, (eds.). *Pain and Injury in Sport Sport: Social and Ethical Analysis.* (London: Routledge, 2006) "Suffering In and for Sport: Some Philosophical Remarks on a Painful Emotion" Chapter 15, Jeffrey P. Fry, "Pain Suffering and Paradox in Sport and Religion" 246-260.

CHAPTER FIVE

ECSTASY AND THE HERO-ATHLETE:

THE ASCESIS OF SPIRITUAL AND PHYSICAL TRANSFORMATION

In the spiritual realm when the athlete reaches the edge and surmises or is transformed by the seeking, by the journey, by the entering into the inner temple within the physical, the athlete encounters self and the experience of pain in it various forms that carried the athlete to and accompanied him or her to transcendence is seen as valuable and necessary.

Underhill in her book *Mysticism*, explores in spiritual terms what is encountered in this realm and gives us a framework for what an athlete hero wisdom figure would return with to share and fortify society. Namely, the hero gains an enlightened understanding of the previously "purposeless suffering" that Armstrong speaks about that is now turned to "purposeful living." This "wisdom" Underhill defines as the ascesis of spiritual and physical discipline. She defines these stages as being in three parts: the Purgative Way, the Illuminative Way and the Unitive Way.[83] She describes in spiritual terms what many athletes talk about in their quest for mind/body perfection. These build upon the ideas and insights we have already explored in Jung's collective unconscious and Campbell's hero myths—so by adding the spiritual component—I believe we are now looking at the whole individual of mind, body and soul. Underhill incorporates the Purgative way, which can be seen as athletic training; the Imitation of the Passion of Christ, as coping with pain, and the tutelage as coaching. Not surprisingly, she sees purgation and illumination

---

83   Underhill, *Mysticism*.

as culminating in ecstasy, the out-of-the-body experience, being beyond oneself, which she labels the Unitive way. Underhill cites the Illuminative way as seeing this suffering as having meaning. All of these elements are also components of how Jung and Campbell see the hero—again, the striking relationship along the continuum of very different disciplines naming and defining things similarly.

And I think if we are to truly understand why athletes go through arduous years of painstaking practice and suffering for those fleeting moments of being a hero, we must add the spiritual component as well. Outside of religion itself, there is a spiritual component to humankind that seeks to find the limits of the mortal, the boundary, the gateway to that which is beyond and athletes are setting a course along that path that we recognize and honor and at times try to follow because we intrinsically know from the kinetic blueprint within, that it has value, wisdom, greatness. So we are willing to pay incredulous amounts of money for the athletes that can throw a strike near 100 mph, win the most Olympic medals *ever*, score a perfect 10 in vault, because these efforts advance us all. And that is critical to understanding why play—in all of its complexity—matters.

Michael Novak reminds us in his landmark study of sport that, "Religions are built upon *ascesis*, a word that derives from the disciplines Greek athletes imposed upon themselves to give their wills and instincts command of their bodies; the word was borrowed by Christian monks and hermits—hence ascetic."[84] We have already touched on Underhill's framework for what an athlete hero wisdom figure would return to society with, namely with an enlightened understanding of the previously "purposeless suffering" that Armstrong speaks about that is now turned to "purposeful living." But what mountaintop did they touch, what Olympus, even if ever so briefly, did they reach? What vista did they gaze upon that sent them returning to us with something meaningful, something lasting that ignites us also? It can't be eternal suffering; no one is really interested in aspiring to that. It has to be the end point, the breakthrough, the

---

84 Novak, *The Joy of Sports*, 29.

edge, the unity of something greater than self—ecstasy.

As I'm using it here, the term ecstasy refers not to a heightened sexual experience but to the athlete's search to go-beyond self, and further, the moment of reaching that edge of self. Endorphins can give athletes a temporary feeling of "the runner's high" but that is a performance experience, not a sustained lifetime goal of transformation. Like Hero swimming to Leander across the Hellespont night after night for love—the dangers, the pain, the sacrifices were accepted—seen as necessary to achieving the goal of reaching the beloved. Such experiences and discipline often lead to transformation of self.

A journey through the collective kinetic unconscious of the athlete's drive to transformation through sport, toward unity with that which is beyond the physical, namely the metaphysical, the spiritual, is achieved in ecstasy. This transformation is part of the myth of the Greek Hero—an athlete, a swimmer—and is seen as a seminal ingredient to attaining wisdom and that certain unitive state with the spiritual that is deemed to be greater than what the athlete was before attaining this ascetic realm.

If we can understand these goals and drives athletes enter into, and indeed seek in their transformative journey—and understand that this path typically involves pain or a type of purgation to gain illumination as necessity of the path which will grant them the final goal of ecstasy, transcendence, then we gain the ability to teach others how to attain the same. Perhaps sport rites achieve this? And that's why we flock, by the droves, to attend them? Ancient athletes cleansed themselves in the Olympics in order to be worthy of performing before the gods, be with the gods. It was a rite, a process, and undertaking to achieve a higher state. Are we moderns really any different?

When we form an aggregate of mystical symbols from the mystical hero tradition as described in Campbell, the spiritual ascesis in Christianity as described in Underhill, and the collective unconscious as described by Jung, we have a compelling argument that these processes exist and influence our search for meaning.

We know that athletes seek to experience the out-of-body experience. We know that runners have named it. We also know that fans can participate in this, recognize the heightened experience of physicality expressed and entered into, as expressed by sport philosopher Michael Novak in his description of the perfect pass: "Tens of thousands of passes are thrown every year... occasionally however, a player or a team executes a play so perfectly—it is as though they cease for a moment to be pedestrian and leap into a realm of the Gods. A great play is like a revelation, the curtains of ordinary life part and perfection flashes for an instant before the eye."[85] And also when he says, "That is why I believe the human race should live. When human beings actually accomplish it, [the moments of beating the impossible odds, the better team, etc., execution of perfection] it is for me as if the intentions of the Creator were suddenly limpid before our eyes: as though into the fiery heart of the Creator we had momentary insight."[86]

The occasion doesn't come often. It is momentary, elusive. But it *was* there! and that is the illumination that brings about change. And once the truth is known that there is more, it can't ever be denied. The gut knows. Transcendence has been experienced and it rains upon society, upon all of us, in our heroes as we seek to join them and transform our meager world.

Transformation. We see it everyday. People are walking for exercise. They are swimming, surfing, rowing, running. We don team emblems, buy NIKE and other brand products by the tens of millions. We want to be like *them!* Humankind takes naturally to the idea of change for the good. We *believe* we can make a difference in our appearance, our health, and our relationships. We believe we can transform ourselves, make our world a better place.

This concept of reaching a point of transformation—or perhaps the belief that we can ready ourselves *for the moment*, right *before* transformation happens is not new to modern society. For thousands

---

85 Novak, 102.

86 Ibid., 159

of years we, as well as the ancients, have been part of a continuum of seeking the next step, the path taken toward the point of change. Doing whatever is necessary to make it happen. Driving ourselves, encountering pain, focusing, committing, at times hoping, praying, Sacrificing. Sometimes individually, sometimes as a group or a team, a tribe, or even a nation. Why? Because we have within us the ability to connect to that which is greater. We know this intuitively. It is one of the reasons that we worship and one of the reasons why we play sports—we are drawn to be in union with something that is greater—to something that makes everything else seem worth it. The high point. The apex. Summit. Ultimate abandonment of self to achieve a higher more heightened experience or illumination—ecstasy.

Continuing on our path along the continuum and examining what the many discourses of people believe, what do the writers say about ecstasy and collective joy? Anthropologist Barbara Ehrenreich states, "There was without question, a tradition of collective ecstasy among the Hebrews."[87] And, that the archaic roots of ecstasy involve play: We can infer that these scenes from prehistoric rock art are depicting dancing figures, which have been discovered at sites in Africa, India, Australia, Italy, Turkey, Israel, Iran, and Egypt among other places....

The ancients engaged in many rituals to achieve personal and also group exaltations. They entered kivas, they had ritualized ceremonies to collectively whip a group into a near frenzied state to achieve a heightened sense. As Ehrenreich states in her book *Dancing in the Streets*, there is a very real infectious, unconscious thrill or state of excitement, joy that wells up within and is tangibly exhibited, to which Ehrenreich asks, "If we possess this capacity for collective ecstasy, why do we seldom put it to use?"[88] And if there is one segment of society that *does* put it to use, or at least tries to, on a daily basis it is those in the pursuit of playing sports, especially those

---

87 Ehrenreich, *Dancing in the Streets.*
88 Ibid., 20.

in pursuit of elite sports—the Olympics, the World Series.

I can remember being at a World Series game where *every pitch*, for the entire game was cheered by the fans. Collectively, the fans were as much into the game and a part of the action as the players. I can remember another time when Pete Rose surpassed Ty Cobb's record with his 2492 base hit—there was a moment—as if the world stood still—of total silence before the explosion, the thrill of celebrating this achievement. Collectively—a stadium of people knew what they were part of and were unconsciously caught up in history. Thrilling! People are jumping up and down, yelling, clapping, stamping feet, throwing confetti. The apex was reached and a release of exuberance followed. Joy.

Ehrenreich says, "For most people in the world today, the experience of collective ecstasy is likely to be found, if it found at all, not in a church or at a concert but at a sports event. Sport sociologist Allen Guttmann and Emile Durkheim have termed this collective expressionism as a "group effervescence that generates a communal solidarity."[89]

Ehrenreich tells us the word ecstasy in the Greek means ex stasis-outside of the body. In the ancient Olympics, the Goddess Demeter was worshiped and the first time the word, ecstasy comes into print is in a story of participants in a ritual celebrating the worship of Demeter.[90] Walter Burkert states, "Because the participants were members of the literate elite, some subjective repots of the ritual's effects have survived. The participants described the experience as purifying, healing, and deeply reassuring; certainly it was transformative. The participants said of the experience, 'I came out of the mystery hall feeling like a stranger to myself,' said one participant of the mystery rites held at Eleusis in honor of the goddess Demeter."

What transformative experience do athletes reach that drive them to seek this moment of separation from self? There was a

---

89   Ehrenreich, 225.

90   Guttmann and Durkheim and additionally Walter Burkett as quoted in Ehrenreich, *Dancing in the Streets.*

collective experience of ecstasy that was recorded and there is reason to assume that what the elite athletes were trying to accomplish in the ancient Olympics was that moment of "god-ness" when they escaped their mortal state and walked among men as gods. Their physical achievements and extreme heightened natures achieved an edge of the state of perfection where they were revered as beyond mortals.

Novak speaks of moments when an athlete reaching the breaking point, the limit and there finds, "recognition of limits is not the only maturation taught by sports. There comes also, at least to some, a sense of their own bodies and attitudes, a sense as if it were from the inside out, quiet, subtle, full of luminosity and peacefulness, beaming from deep within until its rays at last reach consciousness: a sense of inner unity."[91] I believe that it is only when an athlete touches upon this unity he or she is capable of recognizing and meeting— as it were—the Beloved. If we are the body of Christ, would not this unity with self be a unity with the Creator? God is in us, as we are in God and we are in one another? Wouldn't this explain the collective kinetic experience of fans and athletes? The collective kinetic blueprint that unites body, mind and spirit? This journey is so integral to human existence it is the stuff of myth; as we have seen in Campbell's Hero journey, in ancient Greek mythology, and in Jung's collective unconscious—many athletes' desire to seek ecstasy, they seek a unity with something larger than self—the Beloved. Might this explain why one goes willingly into pain, beyond agon in order to achieve transformation? If we can understand these goals and drives of athletes to enter into, and indeed seek this transformative journey—a transcendence typically involving pain, purgation, sacrifice, and eventual illumination which will grant them the final goal of becoming greater than the single self was before, then we can be better coaches, better teachers, maybe even better people.

---

91 Novak, 170.

CHAPTER SIX

CONCLUSION

As a competitive athlete and one who suffered, both voluntarily for the sake of training, and involuntarily in the athletic accident that changed my life, over the years I have tried to share and elaborate on some of my experiences on play and pain. At one conference I was asked specifically about what steps I took that others might follow in order to reach an understanding, meager as it maybe, of the labyrinth of pain and what end it served. What can we extract from these individual experiences to help others? Professor Michael McNamee, in his writing on, "Suffering In and For Sport," asks two questions that stuck in my mind: "What ends are served suffering in and for sport?" And "What qualities attend the suffering?" These two questions kept me awake at night until I could find an answer, at least a partial and perhaps minimal answer in the writing of this book.

In my life, because of suffering, I have at times lost all will to pursue anything—as when I broke my neck and back and spent a decade in the pain control center from which I wrote "Living With Sickness," a book focused on the sojourn of dealing with pain. If it were not for the skilled hands of Dr. Greg and Dr. Raj, I might not have left that space, because in that era I had a Hamlet-like choice— to go on, or not. To be, but to be what? Or not? To be so broken in body and spirit and soul as to merely take up oxygen that someone else might use better? Or live on the tight rope of faith, that there is meaning somewhere if we struggle against enough, faith will reveal and carry us? Tough questions not easily answered without soul searching. Tough questions for an athlete dedicated toward going on, never giving up, hanging tough, playing hurt, etc.

For me, I began to use my discipline of sport, my mental discipline from years of running to go to places inside me where endorphins could carry me past the lactic acid crush, to a better place. For me, part of my searching in this time came through reading every single book the Cincinnati Public Library had on Mount Everest, because it was my ultimate "high" in those terrible years. I played there. I could relate and identify with the climbers lost on the Khumbu Ice Fall, the great glacial calving area that must be crossed to climb Everest from the North Face—for I too was lost among the towering seracs of my mind. As these climbers crossed crevasses of bone shattering depth—I could tremble with them as my bones had been shattered too. The heights they entered, foreign of oxygen they struggled to breathe in—I also knew because my heart V-tacked once, too. Frostbite creeping into finger tips due to exposure to the raw elements—I could relate to as paralysis took over my right side. My daily journeys into MRI machines, over 200 trigger-point injection procedures (there were more but I stopped counting at 200), pain enough to lull you into thinking it would be better to just give-up and die—sit down and rest and succumb to it, enter it as an envelope of relief—was like the climbers finally pushed to the point of exhaustion until they sit and sleep and freeze statuesque, there. They know that to sit and rest is almost certain death. Some succumb. Some take one more step, drive the ice ax one more time— and live. I went to those mountains to escape. I keep an ice ax on my wall from Mont Blanc that I bought years later to remind me to never forget the journey lest I get lost. And on my doorway I have a Jewish mezuzah in reminder to "Remember to Remember God," and for me part of that remembering is in gratitude for the thrill of racing fast, climbing high, being *alive*.

Some of these experiences may not sound like play to you but I believe play morphs and can be relative, maintaining its essential qualities of escape and spontaneity yet growing in encompassment as we grow.

I have tried to examine and explain how along the continuum there are many examples through the ages and across disciplines of this energy we have to play being a connection to the origins of the universe, to the physical nature of self, the collective unconscious, and certainly to society as a whole; to the spiritual nature of human existence, therefore to our higher selves.

So, how can we as fans, as sport philosophers, as coaches, and athletes make a contribution to humankind today? Can we, as C.L.R. James, in his esteemed book, *Beyond a Boundary*, contribute to understanding the personal and cultural struggle of hegemony through the socio-cultural dynamics of cricket? Can we contribute to expand the envelope as to why movies like *Invictus* move us, inspire us as humans—why a rugby game healed the collective unconscious of racial tension? Why it healed a nation and changed the world's outlook on apartheid? This is important stuff!

We have learned that the collective unconscious of scholars, poets, physicists, mathematicians, sport philosophers, writers, athletes, Olympians, theologians, scripture, popes, and sculptors all support a vast collection of descriptions and symbols which reveal that play echoes to us, resonates within us from the origins of the universe to the present and reveals the nature of the energy of play to us, *for us*. These ideas can be linked from the origins of energy in the universe, to a collective unconscious and a collective kinetic blue-print—that explains play phenomena like breakthrough kinesis, explains social and cultural traditions and myths, and carry us to outer realms of the physical, mortal experience to the spiritual heights of ecstasy.

So to answer Michael McNamee's question of what end is served as athletes struggle and suffer in the highest realms of play? What end is served as they take us with us as fans, coaches, on their heroic sojourns? Hopefully, the insight that where we have been, where we are, and where we are going—stems partly from the impetus to play. Play is intended to help us transcend our base nature and *advance us* as part of the energy of the expanding universe. Maybe that's why the Creator blessed us with it. *Play matters, so play as if it matters...*

AFTERWORD⁹²

FROM A VATICAN TALK, NOVEMBER 2009

I would like to thank Fr. Lixey and the Pontifical Council for inviting me to speak and to extend my greeting to your Eminence and esteemed colleagues in this seminar. I am happy to see that the cross of St. Francis of Assisi—the San Damiano Cross—is here in this house with us (The cross hangs on the walls inside of Villa Aurelia.) because thirty years ago I worked in Assisi at the retreat house of Pope John XXIII under Fr. Brunacci!

When I first received the email to come here, I thought it was a practical joke because it was from the Vatican.com. So I called a priest friend in Italy, my friend, Fr. Murray, who is a Franciscan writer and asked him if he sent it? He said no. So my second thought was, wow, I must have done something *really bad* if the Vatican wants to see me—you know, being called to the Vatican for my writing or something. But then, when I opened it and read what it was—an invitation to come here and speak—I was of course very humbled.

I am not a theologian. My background is as a writer, with a Ph.D. in Sport History from Penn State University. I am a coach, and I was a member of the 1993 U.S. National Rowing Team that attended the World Rowing Championships in Racice, the Czech Republic. Any understanding of sport and spirituality I have comes

---

92 Portions of this talk originally printed in, the *Pontificum Consilium Pro Laicis, Sport, Education, Fath: Towards a New Season for Catholic Sports Associations*, Libreria Editrice, Vaticana, 2011.

from my own life experiences. So I must share some of these in order to provide a framework for this understanding. As someone with a Franciscan background and tradition, my telling will be in the form of stories.

That being said, for me, there are places where sport and spirituality intersect. I use my life, *not pridefully*, but in the spirit of the English poet John Keats, who is buried here in Rome. He once said, "Every person's life is a metaphor for the larger life that we represent."

With that, I would like to begin by telling you I was born in Pennsylvania in a small mountain town called Berwick. I was always in the woods. My parents never knew exactly where I was but they always knew I was outside in the woods. I loved to climb and be in the mountains and hike along the ravine we called "The Powder Hole." I just loved being outside and alive. I loved to run, too. At a very early age I wanted to be an Olympic runner and asked my parents if they could get me a coach. We were very poor and didn't have money for that, but they asked a local college student who ran track at nearby Carlisle University if he would coach me. And so I started running at around age 12 or so and have been coached nearly every day of my life in one sport or another since that time. My running course—the marathon course I ran—took me out Bomboy's Lane, down by Mud swamp, and up the hill by Baker's farm.

Running is a great sport—putting one foot in front of the other orders your world and I loved it. I loved feeling the joy it gave me to have this "handedness" and "footedness." I can understand the line from the movie, "Chariots of Fire", when Eric Liddle, the great Scottish Olympic runner, said, "When I run I feel God's pleasure." Those words have stuck with me. Many of you must know what it feels like when you get those endorphins in your system, how you feel alive and full of life! Whether I was out in the woods or running alone out there on that marathon course, I felt there was something with me, something there, something good—a presence—that I started to call The Other. I never felt alone.

I dreamed of being a great runner. I loved all those ancient Greek

Olympic ideals about arête and the pursuit of excellence. I loved all that and aspired to be an Olympian.

And at this time there was also, on another level in my life, something else happening. One night when I was about 10 years old or so, I woke up and I knew, I just knew there was something evil in my room. At this moment I knew, as it was written indelibly in my mind, that evil existed. It is what I call "unwanted knowledge" as it is a burden—especially for a child of ten years old—to know some things.

Anyway, let us move on while keeping this in mind. I next went on to high school where I played five different sports and was captain on four teams. I was in both my high schools sport and academic "hall of fame." I loved sports and I loved playing basketball, skiing, track, gymnastics—I just felt alive!

I went to college and was a double major in fine arts and physical education. To me, sport was like living sculpture so I didn't feel these were diametrically opposing things to study, though most of my professors did. While in college my father had a stroke and I got my first glimpse of a deteriorating body. Everyone in my family was athletic, and now we watched helplessly as our father's condition worsened. Seeing his body change and become blind and crippled by disease really hit me. So much so that I got mad one day and I tore up the Catholic Chapel at Penn State—a small Catholic prayer room where the Blessed Sacrament is kept. I tore off the altar cloth and threw a few flowers against the wall, knocked over a few pews and when I was done, I noticed there was a priest sitting there, Fr. Leopold Kruhl, who later became an Archabbot and my spiritual director. He was one of the Benedictines who was a campus chaplain at Penn State. He said, "Well, do you feel better now?" And I started crying and he held me there in the pew as I cried.

At the time I wasn't a religious person. I avoided church. My mom always had to drag me to church because I preferred to go skiing and hiking or do anything but to go to Mass on Sundays. But after tearing up the chapel, I sat down one night, after my dad had passed away, and took this picture of the Sacred Heart that funeral homes send to the family, and set it on a table and said, "Okay God. I will sit here and listen for one night. If you have anything to say to me, you have one night to say it." That's how arrogant I was!

So I sat there. And I sat there. At around 2 or 3 in the morning all of a sudden I was on the floor and I couldn't get up. I was prostrate on the floor. And I *tried* to get up and as an athlete I was pretty strong. But it was as if I was in the presence of something so huge, so immense, so holy that the floor was the only place I could be. Humble, in worship. And it was as if the wall of my apartment was gone then and I could see way out into space, like the entire universe was there and it was huge and this purple, gold light an *energy and joy* was there in the room and it was just so wonderful I didn't want to leave it. But then it was gone, and I had this strange word in my mind: "Abba". So that morning I went up to see Fr. Leopold and told him what happened. He just smiled and told me to go and buy a Bible and read Romans and of course when I did that, I can say that I established a new relationship with God the Father or "Abba" my other "Daddy" in lieu of my father's passing away.

It was a point-counter-point to the dark angel I saw as a kid. As professor Mike McNamee said earlier—there exists a distinctive energy source, good vs. evil.

So, as a new young Christian, I was out of the starting blocks! I got it. I understood. It was all true. What the Bible said was true. There was good and there was evil. I was on fire to make a difference in the world. I just felt so close to God and I was so happy and bent on celebrating being a Christian and an athlete. It was a great time of happiness for me. But only six months later, I broke my neck and back. I got dropped in a gymnastics accident. I broke T-4 and C-7 vertebrae and had compression fractures at L-4 and L-5. I was hurt. Really hurt. In one instant, all the joy of movement that I had experienced my whole life was gone and I was stilled.

I was told that an injury of that type usually makes you a quadriplegic—but having been an athlete I was told that my strength saved me from this. But I was in incredible pain. I had a tremendous amount of soft tissue damage also. The root of my brachial plexus nerve was torn from the sheath and was rubbing my vertebrae. I couldn't bear the pain. Literally, I just wanted out of the pain, I wanted to "check out", commit suicide, end it all. I was paralyzed for about three months and had pain that felt like someone slipping a hot razor or knife in several parts of my spine and upper shoulder. I couldn't live, I couldn't even feed myself or buy groceries or work.

But somewhere inside I kept searching for an answer... I couldn't believe this "new" God I had just started to believe in would allow this to happen! It was a terrible time of soul searching. I ended up for the next 10 years in the University of Cincinnati Pain Control Center—you have to be really sick to get there. Your quality of life has to be so reduced that there are no more options.

Because of my training as an athlete I was used to pulling it out from deep within, and accustomed to toughness and never giving up. All those things that we teach athletes and that I learned from coaches over the years—discipline, focus, keeping anger in check and between the lines—lines of a basketball court or a rowing venue, whatever. The things we tell athletes are important for the day when life comes around and bites them. They enter into these personal struggles—for me an injury, for someone else the loss of a spouse or death of a child, illness, disease. These are the moments for which what we learn and what we teach shape us as people, not just as athletes, though it is from athletics that skills can help us, toughen us.

I spent years going through procedures, and MRI's, nerve blocks, EMG's that in themselves were also painful at times. And I used many of my skills from my years of sports to help me. I used visualization techniques to take myself far away—all the way back to Mud Swamp and my running trails, until the procedure was over. Pain forces other skills upon you, like patience, dependence and humility. These are important skills too, though they aren't often spoken about in sport practices, and maybe they should be.

But it was very hard to be in the Pain Control Center and one day I told my doctors I had to go to Assisi and talk to St. Francis —a saint I had loved since I was a kid out there walking in the mountains an I loved animals. So, I just had to talk to him and find out why this happened to me. So when I got to Santa Maria degli'Angeli at the base of Mt. Subasio, with Assisi up on the hill, I took off my neck brace and threw it in a trash can and I took off my arm sling as well.

I went to the "pensione" Casa Papa Giovanni—the place I mentioned at the beginning of my talk – where a priest named Don Aldo Brunacci took me in. He was a holy priest who is considered a Righteous Gentile for helping to save the lives of Jews in WWII. I obviously couldn't work much though I could clear the tables with one hand. Mainly I walked in the mountains and went up to the caves where Francis lived and walked the streets and went to the church of San Damiano to talk to him. I wasn't physically healed there—when I left I was still in pain—but I was emotionally healed. I somehow came to understand that God was good and even in my pain He was with me!

While I was in Assisi I started to think about what it means to be a creature of God. I'm sure you know that St. Francis wrote the Canticle of the Creatures. The anthropologist Victor Turner called him a great liminal man—a playful saint! They say that St. Francis would wander the countryside playing an imaginary violin. Through contemplating his life, I started to think about myself as being created by God, that is to say, what it means to be part of creaturehood and to experience peace and play as part of *an intended* work of God's creation. This conviction that play was intentional and that it was part of that energy of God's creation as depicted in the very first pages of Genesis resonated within me as did the energy I felt that night in my apartment in Penn State.

Play also began to intrigue me. Victor Turner also said that all cultures play. Even primitive cultures took time from hunting and gathering to play, so play is an integral part of our creaturely status and was intended by God. God is the essence of joy, and we seek joy in play!

I started thinking about God being at play in creation. The book of Proverbs tells us, regarding Wisdom, that: "When he set the heavens in their place I was at his side, his darling, his delight, *playing* in His presence, *playing* on earth."(Prov. 8:28-31) And of course there are many instances in the Bible that reference play, such as Psalm 107 which refers to Leviathan playing in the sea or those verses in St. Paul regarding sport, etc.

One of the great sport philosophers, Scott Kretchmar, has defined play as, "A state of fundamental pre-rational spontaneity which is freely chosen and entered into for the simple sake of wanting to do so. It is of a nature outside of the reality of the present, yet is equally as real to the players as the present is to the observer."[93] That definition for me contains many elements of the spiritual.

I started thinking of the spiritual energy I experienced that night years before and how the energy we feel inside moving us to play is the presence of God. And I began to see play as the integral urge to participate in what, when it is more complicated and structured, becomes games and then with added competition becomes sports: play, game, sport.

I thought of a Rune poem from 1000 CE that goes something like, "God within me, God without, how can I ever be in doubt? I am the sower and the sown, God's self unfolding and God's own." In other words, when we play we are entering into God, entering into the energy that is God and the Spirit moves through us and we become an integral part of creation and the advancement of humankind.

I started to understand that the pursuit of excellence was a total mind/body/soul achievement, not just mind, body, soul. On any given day, on any field of play someone wins and someone loses. So winning is only a 50/50 proposition. Loosing is only a 50% proposition. But if you pursue excellence—then you are always 100%, you are as high as humans can aspire. Additionally, a great American football coach, Tom Landry, once said that we must learn to lose without losing our dignity. So these are valuable life lessons that athletes practice everyday.

The play philosopher Michael Novak talks about how we can

---

93   R.S. Kretchmar, *Practical Philosophy of Sport*, University of Iowa Press, 1994, p. 210.

share in the creativity of God not only through our work, but also through our play, because play is the exercise of freedom[94] As he notes: "One does not play for the sake of *work*; one plays for the sake of excellence. The point of the excellence is that there is no point."[95]

We recognize excellence when we see it because I believe there is a kinetic blueprint within each of us from when we were with God in the Garden. And this element of God is part of our fabric, part of who we are and when we see a play perfectly executed—we see and recognize something that lifts the players on the field and us to something beyond mortal, closer to the divine. I think as Catholics and as Christians we can see what Michael Novak is talking about when we liken his analogy to our own experiences of how when we see excellence we are drawn to it, we want it, it gives us a moment of unity with the Other who *is* Perfect. The former Cardinal Josef Ratzinger, Pope Benedict XVI himself, considered the free action of play as a sort of effort to return to paradise, as an escape from the wearisome enslavement of daily life.[96]

When I came back to the United States, I was poor and couldn't still really work; I was living in a garage. I mentioned earlier that I was a double major in college so I started to write. I had a great deal of nerve pain, neuralgia in my right hand, so I started to write left-handed. I worked as a free-lance writer and got a piece covering the Cincinnati Regatta, which was the College National Championships.

---

94 Cf. M. Novak, *The Joy of Sports*, p. 231 and 233.

95 Ibid, p. 231.

96 Cf. J. Ratzinger, *Co-Workers of the Truth: Meditations for every day of the year,* Ignatius Press, San Francisco 1992, p. 262 where he states: "One must then ask: What is the fascination of play that it can have equal importance as food? One can answer that by looking back at ancient Rome, in which the cry for bread and circuses was really the expression of a desire for a paradisiacal life, for a life of satiety without effort, and of fulfilled leisure. Because that is what play means: action, that is truly free - without a goal and without a need to do it - while harnessing and fulfilling all of one's personal forces. In this sense, sport becomes a sort of foretaste of Paradise: a stepping out of the slavish earnestness of our daily life and its concerns into the free seriousness of something that should not be serious and is therefore beautiful. In that way sport overcomes daily life. But it has another character, especially with children: It is a training for life. It symbolizes life itself carried forward in freeform manner."

I went to the boathouse, and the Brown University coach was there and said to me, "Susan, you are pretty small and our coxswain is sick; so if you want to jump in the boat, our crew will take you out and you can write from the boat."

And I knew, I just knew as soon as I got in the rowing shell, that this was a way I could finally be an athlete again! I didn't need my body; I only needed my hands and my mind. I had a good deal of watermanship skills and athletic competitiveness and here at least was a way to be an athlete again! I was alive! I wrote the story for the paper and started going back to the boathouse everyday for practice. I started coxing—the person who steers the boat and calls the race strategy—competed on a national lever, and then coached, and finally made the U.S. National Rowing Team and went to the World Rowing Championships. And none of that would have ever happened, if I hadn't broken my neck and back. So God took something terrible and turned it around over time to maybe one of the best opportunities if my life.

Rowing is an interesting sport—it has been a life-giving sport for me and I want to explain how we race. International rowing is done on a 2000 meter long, straight course. We divide the race into four 500 meter segments. The first segment is "the start" where all the crews go off the line at a very high stroke rate and speed, the second segment is called "the settle", when the boats settle into a race pace, the third 500 is an area that I call "never-never land" because it is where your body is switching from aerobic to the anaerobic engine. Here the athletes are in agony—from the ancient Greek word "agon". They are carrying huge amounts of lactic acid in their muscles. In fact, when muscle biopsies were taken at the Olympic Games, rowers had more milli-moles of lactic acid in their quadriceps than the athletes from any other sport. Rowers were second only to cross country skiers. The last 500 metres is "the finish" and the body at this point of the row is suffering, and feels that if it continues, it is going to die. The exertion is so great.

As a Christian, I have started to liken this 2000 meter race, to how we must live our lives in Christ. Think of the cross and Christ's arms outstretched. We start somewhere over here on the left hand of Christ and in our life we are traversing across to the right hand of God, hopefully! The left hand is "the start" and as with the experience that night of God in my apartment, I was on fire! I was out of the starting blocks and heading across and through the body of Christ. The second 500 meters, or "the settle", was for me when I was injured; and here, still moving to the right hand, I reach the center—the very heart of God. This is the moment in my life when I am in the long settle of day-by-day grind of the Pain Control Center. It was a very hard moment in my life and it tried my spirit almost to the point of giving up at times.

Then comes the third set of 500 meters—a moment when we look out beyond our problems to the horizon before us—to others. At this stage in my life I met someone and I fell in love with him. Here came another crisis for me of Olympic proportion where everything I had known or practiced as a Christian, as an athlete—faith, discipline, healing, focus, worship, stick-to-it-tiveness was called into play. Here, in front of me, was someone I loved. But, here also, was a body lying in ruins—the very opposite of my healed person! Here was a person suffering in his own invisible bonds that I could "see." I could see the chains upon him and yet everything I knew as an athlete and a coach and a Christian was not enough to help him! And yet for years, sometimes a lifetime, we pray and we fast and we sacrifice and enter into that "last stretch" of hope and faith—the dark night of the soul—where God seems *not* to hear, nor to answer our prayer, nor to be so powerful. Yet we can only cry, "Abba! Father! Heal him!" as we live only in faith that God is listening. Without faith to bridge the gap these mysteries are like torture. And then maintaining faith can become the hardest race ever rowed.

These are the moments when athletics and spirituality become united in real life, and both body and soul are experienced. As I mentioned in my book on this subject, "Take away the soul and sport is flat, without passion—there is no crucifixion as there is no need for a resurrection. ...Body and soul have a constant and everlasting relationship. Even as in Christ's body in death, it seeks, it waits, to rise. I think that this desire to rise is inherent to athletes and to sport, and in this desire they see something of God."[97]

These are those times when we hit those personal crises—and we all do as I said earlier—whether it may be a car accident, the death of a loved one, a disease. We struggle on, a mere human trying to understand what is seemingly a lack of compassion and action by God to heal and empower us. And *that* is why we coach and what we are really coaching when we stand in front of a team. We are teaching them to have faith, to trust, to believe and to go deep inside —into that energy of God, the soul—and pull out the faith needed in our own hour of need, like Christ on the Cross. Thus, when we are dying to ourselves and our bodies are shifting from the aerobic to anaerobic—without oxygen—in the least part of the "good race," St. Paul tells us to run, we cross the finish line exhausted and lie flat in the boat or flat on the track. We should be completely spent after having become "agon". In doing so, we are like the athlete whose spirit soars in victory but whose body lies flat, completely spent; we leave this earthly plane as our spirit soars, released, because we have given ourselves to one another. Then and only then have we truly entered the mystical body of Christ, and reach the right hand of God—because we have given ourselves.

Play matters—and we should play as if it matters! What we say and how we say things to athletes is important. Play, games, and sports and the lessons learned in them prepare us, if coached properly, for the good race we must run in Christ from the left hand of Christ Crucified, to the right hand. In doing so, we join Christ on the cross as we are called to do and we glorify God in our body and soul.

Play matters and we should play as if it matters because we are playing at the feet of Abba our Father.

---

97   Susan Saint Sing, *Spiritulality of Sport: Balancing Body and Soul*, St. Anthony Press, 2004, p. 111.